Blue-Collar Journal

Books by John R. Coleman

Blue-Collar Journal: A College President's Sabbatical

Comparative Economic Systems

Readings in Economics
(with Paul A. Samuelson and Felicity Skidmore)

The Changing American Economy

Labor Problems
(with George P. Shultz)

Working Harmony
(with Frederick H. Harbison)

Goals and Strategy in Collective Bargaining
(with Frederick H. Harbison)

Blue-Collar Journal:

A College President's Sabbatical

By John R. Coleman

J. B. Lippincott Company
Philadelphia and New York

U.S. Library of Congress Cataloging in Publication Data

Coleman, John Royston, birth date
  Blue-collar journal: a college president's sabbatical.

  1. Coleman, John Royston, birth date 2. Labor and
laboring classes—United States—1970— Case studies.
3. College teachers—Leaves of absence—Case studies.
I. Title.
HB119.C57A3   378.1'1'0924 [B]   73–21902
ISBN–0–397–01030–3

To
the memory of
my mother and father
who would have understood
how much
there was to learn
from those I met

Foreword

In the spring of 1973, I took a leave from my job as a college president. There were no strings attached. I could do whatever I chose for months on end. I had secretly known what I wanted to do if ever such a chance came along; now I had to discover whether I was serious about it.

What I wanted to do was to try my hand at manual work, for reasons more complex than I pretend to understand. I only know that, every time in recent years when I looked ahead to some time out, my thoughts turned to seeking and holding blue-collar jobs. The idea of breaking out of what I normally do and of taking up different roles for a while was so compelling that I would have felt cheated had I done anything less.

This is a record of what I did once I pulled out of the driveway of my house. The journal covers eight weeks. It omits the first week when I worked with friends of thirty years' standing, Pat and Russell Best, on their dairy farm in Ontario. That week conditioned me for physical work; thirteen hours a day in a milk shed, cow barns, and the woods have that effect. It omits the last weeks of my leave when I fulfilled a quite different dream by spending a week in Florence and a night each at Vienna's Staatsoper and at Milan's La Scala.

From the start I realized how fortunate I was in being able to get away at all, and in being able to leave without telling anyone where I was going or what I planned to do. I am divorced. I consider my children old enough and independent enough—and they consider me so—that I can disappear for some time without their having to worry about me. The college board of trustees and my administrative colleagues were trusting enough not to push me with questions about how I proposed to use the time out. And I had a paycheck going into the bank each month to meet the tuition, insurance, utility, and tax bills that found their way to the house, however far away I might be.

I did not tell anyone about what I planned to do with my sabbatical because I was afraid the response would be what part of me also said: "Jack, that's crazy." No reply to that charge would sound convincing, and I felt that my orthodoxy and my quest for respectability would take over at that point. I would probably end up using my leave to do some sort of survey of recent developments in liberal arts education, and it would no doubt be published somewhere through the help of friends in editorial posts. But it wouldn't be worth much because I'm not an original thinker on that subject. All in all, I thought, it was better to keep to myself the urge to reenter the blue-collar world for the first time since 1945. Let me see if I am willing to go where I want to go. And then let me see if I can explain it afterward.

I started the journal immediately after the week on the Bests' farm. It was to be just for me, and perhaps someday for my children. The more I wrote and the more I experienced, the more I wanted to share my time out with others who might have a similar desire to break the lockstep for a while. In the months after my leave ended, I polished and expanded the entries I had made myself sit down to write every night without fail. I have changed the names of the people with whom I worked to protect their privacy; I have done the same with company and place names where necessary.

This book is dedicated to my parents. But it could have been dedicated to Walter Mitty. He too would have understood.

JOHN R. COLEMAN
Haverford College
October 1973

One

Friday, February 16, 1973   *Atlanta, Georgia*

The drive from Philadelphia to Atlanta seemed
long, no matter how good the road was. I hadn't
counted on Georgia's being so far from home. I was
keyed up, and the miles went by as slowly as they
did for my children years ago on our vacations,
when, one hour after we started the all-day drive
to Maine, they asked, "Are we almost there?"

The sky was still dark when I pulled out of the
driveway of my campus home this morning. Even in
dim light, the big old house looked inviting. I knew
that I would miss its comfort and space—the books
and records in the library downstairs, the paintings
in the living room, the kitchen where it is fun both
to cook and to talk, and the big cluttered desk in the
study upstairs.

In addition to the car, I brought two hundred
dollars in travelers checks with me and a gasoline

13

credit card. The checks were to tide me over until I got a paycheck. The credit card was to let me get home even if I ran out of money for food and lodging. I had a duffel bag full of clothes, a few kitchen supplies, a box of books, a portable radio, and my camera. I also brought my social security card—I had already decided to use my own name—but nothing else. The rest of my past had to stay home. I would invent an earlier work history as I went along.

The strongest feeling today was one of freedom. Just how much freedom there was became clear as soon as I reached the main road running past the campus. I could head in any direction I chose. I stayed with my original plan and headed south, but I felt freed just in knowing that I could have changed my mind on the spot.

I had agreed with my board of trustees that I would spend a preliminary month out of the president's office but still working on college affairs. I had turned the presidency over to the provost on New Year's Eve (that was freedom, too!) and had set out two days later to travel around the country seeking funds for the college. The money-raising had gone well, I thought. And the trips had given me a secret bonus. In each city in the eastern half of the country, I had read the Help Wanted ads in the local paper. (I had done that in my hotel rooms; no man in a business suit ever reads employment ads in public.) I had been scouting the job markets to prepare for today. Atlanta had come out of that casual survey as the most promising place to begin;

there was enough growth evident there to mean labor shortages in a number of fields. I had never been in the South for more than a few days at a time. Atlanta was, therefore, almost unknown to me, so this would be a change in itself.

The last time I asked anyone for a job was in 1949 when I applied for an instructorship in economics at M.I.T. I thought I had something to sell then. Today I wondered what I had to sell in the unskilled labor market. I am fifty-one years old, have done no manual work to speak of for almost thirty years, and have brought no references along to use. The only assets seem to be that I'm in good health, I'm energetic (I don't play competitive sports, but I run, swim, and skate), and I get to work on time. Will those be enough? It will all depend on how tight the labor market is. I know that I dread the thought of being turned down.

It was 6:00 in the evening when I got into Atlanta, and time to eat. I passed up the restaurants I would ordinarily have sought out and headed for a diner on the outskirts of the downtown area. There was a copy of the morning's *Atlanta Journal* still on sale. I skipped the front pages and turned to the classified ads. The Help Wanted columns didn't look as promising as they had last month, particularly for outdoor work.

The only choices appeared to be yardman, construction worker, or general laborer. Yardman was a risky job; the weather was cold for Atlanta (18°) and work could be spotty. Just a few days of bad weather and I'd have trouble supporting myself on my earnings. Most building construction ads called for experience; I thought it would probably be better if I toughened up elsewhere before I tried to make out in that league. That left the simple classification of "laborer."

Four ads were similar. Someone was paying a lot to get clean water into, and dirty water out of, the Atlanta area. This one stood out:

> "Laborers. Sewer and water line con-
> struction. Transportation furnished. Call
> MU 2-0736 after 7 P.M."

It was those words "after 7 P.M." that caught my eye. I had expected to use the night to build up my courage to start making calls at dawn. But here was a chance to get hired right now. Seven o'clock was drawing near; it was time to act.

I finished my hamburger and went to the telephone booth outside. I walked up and down with a dime in my hand for some time. In part, I was nervous about the work; in part, I wanted to avoid seeming too anxious by calling too soon. It was 7:05 when I dialed.

A male voice answered.

"Hello. My name is John Coleman. I'm calling about your ad for sewer laborers. Could you tell me about the job?"

"I start them at two-seventy-five an hour."

That was that. Obviously I needed more questions.

"What's the work like?"

"At this time of year it's dirty, and sloppy, and wet, and cold. It's a lousy job any way you look at it. Are you interested?"

"Yes. I'd like to try."

"What kind of work have you been doin'?"

"I've just come here from Pennsylvania. I used to be in sales. [That was true for a college president by a small stretch of the imagination.] But I got tired of it. [That would surely be true if the first statement were literally true.] So I've been working as a laborer for a while. [Completely false, except for that warm-up week on the dairy farm.]"

"Well, like I say, I start you at two-seventy-five. If you're any good, I'll move you ahead. Some of my men get three-and-a-half. Some get four."

"Do you want to meet me before you hire me?"

"No. Just come ready for work. Dress warmly. We'll supply boots when you get wet work."

"Is it a hard-hat job?"

"It's supposed to be. But I've stopped givin' them out. The men won't wear them, even though it's for their own good."

He gave me detailed instructions on how to find the job site and told me to be ready for work at 7:30 on Monday. I asked if I could start tomorrow.

"All right, if you need the money."

"I'll be there at seven-thirty. What's your name?"

"Gus Reed. R-E-E-D."

"Thank you, Mr. Reed."

That was all. I felt relieved at being hired on my first try—and without even being asked my age.

17

I didn't sleep very well—partly from excitement, partly from doubts about whether I could do the day's work at 51.

I spent the night at a motel downtown. The rate was more than I wanted to pay, but I didn't feel up to an after-dark search for something cheaper. Maybe I was also trying to ease myself into this new life one step at a time.

It was 5:45 this morning when I came down to check out at the motel desk. The day was biting cold, not at all what I expected the South to be like. Luckily, I had brought warm clothing with me to be ready for whatever came along. I wore thermal underwear left over from a horseback and climbing trip into the Canadian Rockies three years ago. On top of that were an old shirt and pants and a sweater that had been a home to many moths. Over that, in turn, I had gray coveralls that I had bought new for the trip. I had laundered them twice to make them seem worn; I didn't want to look as if I had come straight from Sears. On my feet were the high, laced rubber boots that had served me well on the dairy farm.

The clerk at the motel desk looked surprised at my clothes. That's not the way the Travelodge guests normally dress.

"Going to work?" he asked. I decided I had passed the appearance test.

"Yes."

"What do you do?"

"I'm starting today with a sewer company."

"On a cold morning like this?"

"Yes."

"You poor shit!"

It occurred to me that he could be right. I paid the bill, packed my gear in the car, and headed for the northeast drive out of town. There were very few cars on the road at that hour on a cold Saturday morning. Just us working folks, I thought.

A Waffle House diner on Route I-95 had only a handful of customers. They were dressed about the same as I was. None of them gave me more than a glance. I don't know now why I expected they would. I ordered bacon and eggs, the way I had seen workers in movies do, and bought a ham sandwich to take along for lunch just in case. I even ate the grits that came with the eggs; I was determined to go the whole way in this role.

It was still not 7:00 when I got close to the job site. It was just outside Atlanta where a county road intersects Route I-285. I rode up and down in the area for twenty minutes or so putting in time and even considering the possibility of keeping right on going.

At 7:20, I parked at the site and got out. There was a large, leveled, and graded field beside me. A sign informed the passersby on I-285 that a self-service storage warehouse would soon rise on part of that land. Around the field's edge, there were to be sewer and water lines. That was the job I was heading for.

A construction trailer, a shed, a couple of portable toilets (names like "Johnny-on-the-Spot" and

"Port-o-John" always leave me wishing my name were Fred), a few pieces of construction machinery, and piles of pipe lengths were about all there was to be seen above the ground. The site was generally neat. I assumed that it looked the way the boss wanted it to look.

I shouted to a man warming up the engine of a backhoe to ask if Gus Reed were around. He pointed to the only other person to be seen; that man too was warming up a machine. This second man was in his early forties, redheaded, stocky, and with a wind-cut face pleasant and tough at the same time.

I introduced myself to him, half holding out my hand for a shake. There was no response.

"Fine. I'll get to you in a few minutes." I waited awhile. I recalled having read in the personnel books from which I taught many years ago about the importance of orienting new employees to the job. "Their first impressions may be lasting ones," was the message. I wondered how the orientation would proceed here.

A man appeared, driven to the site by an attractive young blonde. He was no more than twenty-two or so, white, with longish hair and dressed in mud-and-grease-covered fatigues and rubber boots. I didn't hear what he said to Gus, but I heard all that Gus said in reply.

"What the shit! I don't give a fuck what you thought. If you couldn't get the truck started, you should have fuckin' stayed with it instead of gettin' your pussy to drive you the fuck out here. Now get the hell back there and get the fucker started."

A few more men, white and black, drifted in.

One man who made it at 7:45 got a short greeting from Gus. "Good afternoon, Robert. Are you sober?"

Robert neither smiled nor replied. He just looked plain weary. Perhaps he was fifty-five, but his black, deep-lined face made it hard to tell.

There were orders to each man to start on a specified task. It was 7:50 before Gus turned to me. "Get a shovel out of the trailer and get in that ditch. Just follow the backhoe along and throw all the shit that it misses up on the bank."

I chose a long-handled spade from the trailer's rack and climbed into the trench which the backhoe had already made. The orientation was over. My first impressions were already formed.

The work looked easy enough. The dirt was loose, and the banks of the trench were not too high. It's just that there was so much of the stuff. After tossing the fiftieth shovelful out of the five-foot-deep trench, I suddenly thought that my heart might not like this too much. How many times had I read of men in their fifties dying while shoveling snow? But there was no turning back now unless I had the gall to get out of the ditch and walk away. I was a ditchdigger, for better or worse.

Gus was rather easy on me. He pointed to where the jackhammers had ripped up a road which the sewer line was to cross. The curbs on both sides of the road were left intact.

"John, take your time but shovel out that shit from under the curbs. Tunnel through from both sides so that we save the curbs."

No problem, I thought. But the six-foot-thick walls of clay there were packed hard. Sometimes I

shoveled from a stooped position. Sometimes I had
to kneel in the mud to get further under the curb.
Either way the shovel hit the same unyielding clay
with a thud. Only a small amount of dirt fell away
with each try.

Some sort of supervisor or engineer walked by.
(I realized I didn't even know the name of the
company I was working for, much less who the
key personnel were.) He smiled down at me from
the ridge, a patronizing smile.

"That must be the warmest place to be right
now," he said.

I agreed it was comfortable. There was no need
to argue just now. Both what he said and how he
said it carried me back more than thirty years to a
summer job as a college student. I was working on
the "bull gang," the common labor pool for International Nickel Company in my hometown in Canada. For some days I was part of a four-man crew
flushing out the sewers under the smelter's concentrating plant with high-pressure hoses. We spent
much of each day down in the sewers, playing our
hoses on the beds of silt that had built up over the
years. Most of the dirt was ore and clean enough on
that account, but naturally there was more than that
flowing through the ducts and splashing up on us.
I came up one day, my rubber suit and probably
my face covered with the muck from below and my
nose full of the stench of the job. A supervisor I
knew in the town was standing at the top, grinning
down at me as I climbed out of the manhole into
the hot summer air outside.

"It must be nice and cool down there," was

all that he said. I bit my tongue and didn't ask if he wanted to swap jobs. Few people know how to talk to a man in a ditch. I suppose talking down just comes naturally in the circumstances.

One of my hopes in such a job as this was to have long talks with manual workers. I had imagined myself learning much more than I had already read about the blue moods that are said to go with their blue collars these days. But I saw how naïve this was at once. There was no talk while I dug. There was no one there but me. The trench was so narrow that both shoulders sometimes rubbed against the muddy walls during a full swing of the shovel. And even if there had been someone near me, the jackhammers tearing up the roads we crossed and the backhoe making the trench ahead ruled out any talk other than shouts.

Shovel away. The talk can wait.

I stopped thinking about my heart. I decided that, if it were going to give out, it would have done so by now. I knew now that it was the muscles that would give me more trouble. They began to ache long before 10:00. I breathed hard after some of the sustained lifting of load after load above my head. But I felt safe, even happy in a way.

I thought I heard Gus say to someone up above, "John's a good worker." But the backhoe operator was also named John, and I didn't look up to see which one of us Gus was looking at. I figured that such compliments would be rare, and it would be well to grab any that floated around loose.

With the tunnels under the curb done, the long ditch stretched out before me. It might not have seemed so long from the street level, and certainly wouldn't be long to anyone whizzing by in a car, but the view from the trench was of banks of mud that stretched on and on. The backhoe had moved rapidly while I was digging away at the packed clay. How many thousand shovel loads of loose dirt had it left behind for me? And would I ever catch up to that machine again?

In the work I do as college president, there are only two tasks that require doing the same thing over and over again for any sustained period of time. One is shaking hands at commencement and parents' day (a happy task); the other is signing thank-you notes to alumni contributors (a very happy task). But both the lines of people waiting to be greeted and the pile of notes waiting to be signed have definite ending points: I know when I'll be done with them. The ditch today didn't seem to have an end. As fast as I cleaned up one foot of it, the backhoe made at least one more foot of it ahead.

The soil was uniform in its reddish color, and each load looked almost exactly like the one before. Now and then there was a rock in it, which made for a bit of variety, particularly in the effort it took to get the load shoulder high. For the rest there was almost no break in the morning's routine.

However, one five-minute break was a surprise. About 11:00 Gus bought us sticky buns and hot coffee from a passing canteen truck.

In his autobiography, *Inishfallen, Fare Thee Well*, Sean O'Casey tells of the last days in his mother's life. This woman had had thirteen children and a life of hard labor and little money. Sean and she lived together at the end, now quite penniless. As she lay on a flea-infested sofa with a few scraps of blanket over her, he brought her some tea, and she told him, "If you go on pamperin' me this way, you'll spoil me forever from doin' anything again."

And here was Gus pampering us. Where would it all end?

Except for that short break and two trips to the portable toilet (very cold and drafty, but clean), I wasn't out of the ditch all morning. I longed for lunch. When noon came with no letup in the work, I let myself believe that Saturday was probably a half day and that we'd close up at 1:00 for the weekend.

At 12:30, Gus called a short break. Almost everyone got in cars and sped away. A black laborer who looked about my age and I were left alone by the road. A long way behind us were eight men who had been rented from a part-time labor agency in town to work for the day; they raked lazily by the road but didn't seem to be treated by anyone as part of our crew. So far as I could see, they didn't eat.

The one remaining laborer and I introduced ourselves.

"I'm Al."

"I'm John."

We shook hands, the only time I did that today. He ate his sandwich and I ate mine, as we sat on a sewer pipe near the trench.

Al's speech was soft and his manner the same. His dark work clothes and brimmed hat matched his skin. He told me about years as a longshoreman in San Francisco and then about his move to Atlanta "because there were just too many of us on the docks to live." He had worked at this sewer job only a little longer than I. He was more attracted by the words in the Help Wanted ad about "Transportation furnished" than by the ones that caught my eye. Al had no car. The only way he could get from Atlanta's black neighborhoods to a job like this would be in the company's truck or car.

The rest of the crew soon returned from a diner nearby. It was just half an hour after the lunch break began that Gus appeared in the trailer door.

"Let's go."

The afternoon was easier. I was put on top of the newly dug trench to hook water-pipe lengths for Gus Reed, who was now serving as a craneman. My job, once a heavy length was safely chained to the backhoe's long arm, was to guide that pipe to the trench, where two men laid it and joined it to the one laid before. "Guided" is too strong a term for what I did. At best, I kept the cast-iron tubes from swinging too wildly in the air on the trip from the pile to the trench. Had I been in the ditch, I'd have wanted a hard hat—and a comprehensive insurance policy too.

The pipelayers were Stanley and Robert. I learned that by keeping my ears open and not because anyone told me their names. Robert was the weary-looking older man who had been asked if he was sober this morning. His work in the afternoon sun showed that he was a bull as a worker, sober or not. As a pipelayer, it was his job to get each length laid just right, with the joint to the next length suitably tight. That task often required straining on a long, heavy steel bar to push the pipe into place. The sweat on his brow and the dripping stream from his nose told their own story of a life of hard work. Robert talked little but worked very hard.

Stanley was the man who had got the stream of abuse when he first arrived in his girlfriend's car. That early-morning abuse was repeated by Gus over and over throughout the day. It was worst when Stanley was laying pipe with Robert, right under Gus's nose.

"Goddamnit, Stanley, I've just learned another thing you can't do—lay water pipe. If you'd stop fuckin' that pussy of yours and get some sleep, maybe you'd learn to do somethin'. You're the shittiest fucker I've had on this job."

With every pipe length, it was the same. "Goddamnit, Stanley, put some fuckin' muscle behind that bar and let's get some pipe laid."

In the end, Stanley got a rest of a sort when one particular length of pipe proved stubborn about linking up with the next.

"Goddamnit, Stanley, get out of that trench and take a fuckin' long rest. You'll never amount to nothin' nohow. Never will."

Stanley stood and watched, without a word or much change of expression on a handsome face. I was scared, imagining when I would feel Gus's wrath. I wouldn't be on the job long enough to be broken in as a pipelayer, but I felt sure there would be other situations where Gus would come down on me hard.

Gus hopped out of the backhoe's cab and into

the ditch to take over the bar. By now, the red of his face was approaching that of the jacket he wore all day. But that pipe length didn't go in one bit better for him than it had for Stanley. How would he explain that?

"Goddamnit, Stanley, do you see what the fuck you've done? You've gone and got us all upset. You're a menace just by bein' around."

That's the way it went most of the afternoon.

Eventually I was ordered to shovel asphalt and clay with two men from the group of eight laborers hired from the contract agency in Atlanta. These men are the equivalent in manual occupations of the Kelly Girls in office work. I asked one of them how these agencies work.

"Simple. It's about the same way they buy and sell cows. You get there about five-thirty or six in the morning and sit on one of their bare benches until a call comes. The guy who runs it says, 'O.K., you—and you—and you.' He crowds the gangs for two or three jobs into the back of an old panel truck—no windows, no heat. Then some young punk drives us out to the jobs, drops us off, gets a receipt for us, and disappears. If he's any good, he finds out when to pick us up again. If he isn't, we just wait. We do what we're told for the day. Then it's back into the truck, except it smells more by then, and back to the hiring hall. We get paid each night—and if we're smart we get drunk right after. Same thing the next day. You never know what you'll be doing. And nobody gives a shit anyway."

He thought they were getting $1.50 an hour, but he wasn't sure. He had no idea what the agency got. Their shoveling showed the low pay, low esteem, and low morale in their work. With a new boss every day of their lives, they saw no gain in impressing any one of them with a burst of energy. Now that I was working beside two of them, I couldn't decide whether to slow down to their pace as a way of getting along with them or to keep up the morning's pace as a way of getting along with Gus. As a result, I think I went back and forth from slow to fast and puzzled everyone in turn.

No one had mentioned anything about quitting time. I assumed now that it would be 4:00, making this an eight-hour day. But that hour came and went without any signal from Gus. So did 5:00. My shovel was fully a part of me now, just like my legs and arms. Most of what we had to show for the day was already buried beneath the ground. The trench was gone and so was the pipe. Only the newly raked ground would tell a passerby that we had done a job there.

It was 6:00 when Gus called it a day.

"John, go in that truck with all that equipment. You might as well learn where all that shit goes at night."

Everything had a neat place in the trailer. There was no way of making a mistake in stowing it for the night.

Gus and Stanley were talking down the road at some length. Or rather Gus was talking. Only the four-letter words and the strong gestures carried as far as the trailer.

At last Gus came to me. "See you Monday. This wasn't our usual work. We don't often lay lines along the highway. Usually we're over in the swampy stuff. Someday soon you'll be up to your ass in mud. Seven-thirty Monday."

I took off my coveralls before I got in my car. They were muddy enough for one clean day.

Stanley was standing alone as I drove away. He had told me he rode home with Gus each night. I wondered what they talked about.

I had no zest for looking for a place for the night. I had read rooming-house ads in yesterday's paper, but they were all downtown. I'm lazy enough to prefer living near the job; more than five years of stepping out of the door of a fine old home and crossing two small fields beneath the trees on the way to my office have spoiled me for commuting. I had no idea tonight where rooms could be found in the suburbs, and I was too weary to try to find out.

I remembered passing a motel this morning that advertised rooms for "$8 a day." Compared with the prices I usually paid, that seemed a steal. It was only after I registered that I realized eight dollars represented almost three hours of labor today. But at least I could now have a bath, eat, and get into bed.

I ate at a diner nearby. Heavily. Potatoes and bread and even pie—items I don't usually buy. But tonight they seemed just right. The bill came to almost another hour of my work.

Last night I started this journal with a firm resolve to write something, no matter how brief, each day. Whatever strength I have now to keep so new a resolve comes from the knowledge that tomorrow is a day off.

30

I slept almost nine hours without waking.

My back was stiff and sore. Only as the day went on did I think I might be able to use it again. I discovered muscles in my arms and legs that I had never known existed before. Two days ago I prided myself on walking fast and tall. Today I prided myself on walking at all.

The chambermaid who came in to clean told me her husband was as young as she was. "But he works outdoors on construction. It's hard work, and when he comes home all he wants to do is sleep." I told her I understood.

I have decided to stay on at this motel. Its nearness to the job and the joy of its bathtub at the end of the day are enough to persuade me to stay. I see that this means I am making only part of the transfer from my usual life to that of an hourly man. Still, it's a big change for me.

The cost bothers me, I admit. I have those two hundred dollars in travelers checks, but I promised myself to put that amount back in my checking account at home out of my earnings on the road. To keep that pledge and to avoid having to call my oldest son for money, I have to live within what I earn and set some money aside.

I am assuming that yesterday is about what I can expect in the weeks ahead. With so long a work day, there must be overtime pay. That lets me relax a bit about eight dollars a day for the room and almost four dollars for food. I obviously can't cook in my room, but I can buy cold meats, bread, fruit, and cokes and make my lunches there. That leaves breakfast and dinner to buy. I have an assortment of clothes that should carry me through two months with ease. I have what I wore yesterday, an old pair of jeans, a denim jacket that I think belongs to my second son, Paul, a couple of work shirts from hiking trips, and two pairs of boots. Since there is so little I have to buy, I should be able to meet the budget with ease. This may be a small amount in comparison with what I usually spend—but it's a great deal more than many Americans see in a week. Whatever I learn now about the world of work, I can't pretend I'm learning what it's like to live at the bottom of the heap.

Monday, February 19

We worked from 7:30, a little before sunrise, until 7:00, a little after sunset. My car lights were on when I drove to work, and they were on when I drove home. Saturday had apparently been a short day.

I was on one job the entire day. A different part of Gus's crew took over extending the water line on which we had worked on Saturday. I was put on the opposite side of the road with a small gang that was to lay sewer pipe. The trenches now were deeper, about nine feet as against five for the water line. They were carefully sloped so that gravity could guide the sewage's flow.

Gus acted as craneman and exhorter for the job. He oversaw everything that we did, never stopped prodding us on, still managed to keep his eyes on the rest of his men on the site, and had time left over for brief fisticuffs with a passing truck driver who complained that one of our trucks blocked the road. I would never have considered getting into a fight with Gus; the truck driver probably wished he hadn't thought of it either.

We had two men laying the heavy clay pipes in the ditch. One was Robert, the stolid, steady man I had watched lay pipe before. With him was Langston, a taller, much younger, lighter-skinned black. His every movement was swift and free, and he furnished a line of reveries and gags that kept pace with the work he did. His worn and faded denims would have been the envy of our well-to-do students. Robert and Langston seemed to have little in common but their race, yet they worked as a team in a way that showed they had done this together before.

I was on top of the trench. My sole job was to shovel dirt back into the ditch to give a first covering to the pipe before a tractor operator came along and finished burying the line—though I never did figure out why it was necessary to do the hand job at all. The tractor did its work with such speed that it seemed idle for me to be messing around with that first layer of dirt. I had heard someone on Saturday say that Robert had been a pipelayer longer than anyone else on the job, so I asked him at one point why I was doing what I did.

"That's just the way we do it," he explained.

I don't suppose I could have done the job much

better even if I had learned what it was about. It's just not something that can be done badly or well. Slow and fast were the only options open to me.

There is a lot of time for counting on a job like that. I kept track of the shovel loads of dirt needed to bury each of six lengths of the pipe and averaged them out to ninety or so. We buried over one hundred lengths—nine thousand shovelfuls for the day.

I tried different techniques for doing the job. Left hand on top of the shovel. Right hand on top. Swing to the left. Swing to the right. When any lifting at all seemed too much for my arms, I tried just pushing whatever dirt lay near the ditch's edge into the hole. There wasn't enough dirt there to make much difference, so it was back to lifting again.

Eleven solid hours of it, broken only by lunch, two trips to the canteen truck for milk and the toilet for relief, and an occasional stint pushing new pipe lengths into the pit for Robert and Langston to lay.

I quickly found that I couldn't lift the clay pipe lengths alone. I had seen a worker named Braden do it easily when the pipes were laid along the embankment this morning. Braden was a white ex-Marine and so powerfully built that he almost seemed a match for Gus. It didn't surprise me that he could swing those pipes to his shoulder and down again without a crash. But when a much smaller man, Carl, filled in for a while for Gus on the backhoe and then swung a pipe length onto his shoulder with almost the same ease, I felt underprivileged.

Gus saw me try to lift one of the lengths, fail,

and have to push it across the ground to the ditch's edge.

"Better hit the Wheaties, John," he called.

"Give me a week," I replied. But I knew that might not be enough.

At one point in handling the pipe, I smashed the watch on my arm. Then I understood why I was the only one who seemed to know the time before that. Watches and pipeline work don't mix.

After that I tried to tell the time by the sun. My shadow took forever to lengthen on the dirt pile where I worked. It was as if time stopped just because the watch I inherited from my father had stopped. We had seen fleets of trucks go out early in the morning from the electric utility down the road. I kept watching for them to return for the night. Eventually they came in, stirring up clouds of dust that blew in our faces. That meant our quitting time too shouldn't be far away—but it was. The sun clung stubbornly to its place in the sky. There were trees at the far edge of the field, and I waited for the sun to edge closer to their tops and kept myself from looking up from the dirt for, say, two full pipe lengths. When I did look up, I couldn't see that the trees and the sun were one bit closer together.

The men on the utility trucks must be home, showered, and beered by now, I thought. Maybe I chose the wrong job.

At last the sun gave up and yielded to the trees. Once it did, darkness came with merciful swiftness. We put the last tools away by the light from the trailer.

Stanley told me with a smile in one break that

Gus was always after his ass. The abuse seemed to roll off him. I wondered how. Two days on the job told me I couldn't take that treatment. I needed some bit of encouragement.

Gus finally made the day for me in the last minutes, as we were cleaning up in the semidarkness. "John, clean away that shit around the hydrant. Please."

Please.

I'd have done it with my toothbrush.

Tuesday, February 20

I count. My name went on a time card today.

Gus had to ask my last name in order to put it on. Last names are almost unknown here. I think Goddamnit is Stanley's other name, but beyond that Gus is the only man whose full name I know.

The boss told me that my first job this morning was important in determining whether or not the water line would eventually pass its pressure tests. I spent an hour putting rubber rings in the flanges of the eight-inch and six-inch pipe lengths. Each ring had to fit perfectly, and there was to be no dirt at all in the seal. To get the pipe ends clean took a cloth and a lot of blowing. The blowing had the effect of transferring most of the reddish brown dust from the pipe end to my face, but I felt almost semiskilled for that hour. The feeling disappeared later in the day when I saw the pipes deringed and cleaned all over again because of the dirt they gathered as they bumped along the ground on their way to the trench for laying.

For most of the day, Stanley, Langston, and I were a pipelaying crew under the direction of the project engineer. Dick is the only college man here; he's a Cornell civil engineer. Where everyone else seems to fit in with the pipes, machinery, mud, and tools of the trade, he just doesn't look quite right. He has a gentleness and a quizzical look that would go better at Haverford than it does here. Even his few obscenities seem out of place. Most of the time Dick works the transit and sets up the laser beam used in getting the sewer line straight and properly sloped. Today he operated the backhoe too, but with more determination than style.

The work seemed easy by comparison to the trench shoveling. And there was time for fun. The kidding that went back and forth among the four of us flowed easily from our work together. I was happy working with each of these men; I thought they enjoyed the day too. I even thought that we were making good headway. We had laid over eight hundred feet of sewer by sunset.

Then Gus called us into the trailer at checkout time. The entire crew was there to hear him. He proceeded to lay us low.

"You call eight hundred feet in a fuckin' day a good job? Why, Ronnie and me and two colored fellows from the part-time agency once laid nineteen hundred feet in one day. And once when Robert was so drunk I had to grab him by the fuckin' seat of the pants to keep him from fallin' in the ditch, we laid twice *that* much. You ask Robert."

37

Robert said nothing. He didn't even smile, although I think he heard.

"The trouble with you guys is you're all ironheads. You don't think. You use your muscles and your feet when you should use your heads. Use the machines. Let them do the fuckin' work. But use them right. Get the fuckin' cable from the machines straight up and down when you're tryin' to place pipe or you're wastin' your fuckin' time. And my fuckin' money too. I get two dollars a foot for layin' that pipe. You laid eight hundred feet. How do we make money that way? The damn machine alone is worth forty dollars an hour.

"It all comes down to the supervisor. Dick, you did a shit of a job with this crew. How can you boast about it?"

"I didn't," was Dick's quiet reply.

"You've got to plan ahead, Dick. You're always thinkin' an hour or two behind where you're workin'. I'm an hour or two ahead. That's the difference between a hundred-dollar-a-week man and a thousand-dollar-a-week man."

And on, and on.

Gus's lungs match his muscles; he seemingly cannot tire. Yet, strangely, he didn't seem all that angry as he dressed us down. It was disconcerting, too, that his sons, about nine and seven, climbed all over his shoulders while he talked. They grinned. We didn't.

"And who the hell moved that stake to make it look as if you had come to the end of the line? I know damn well it doesn't belong there—and you guys ain't finished by twenty feet or more. Who's the shit that tried that trick?"

We had all seen it moved. But no one squealed.

When I got back to my room, I rather liked what I saw in the mirror. Two days outdoors in the Georgia sun had given me a healthier tan than I had ever had before. It was reddish brown and remarkably even. Unfortunately, almost all of it came off in the bathtub or on the towel.

Wednesday, February 21

I was happy driving to work this morning. The muscles were no longer as sore as before, I knew some of the men I'd be working with for the day, and I felt that I was beginning to fit in with the crew. At the diner where I had breakfast once again, I felt that I was fully a part of the blue-collar world. Two gas station attendants, a schoolbus driver, and the short-order cook knew mine was a familiar face and said hello. I was proud of the fact that I would probably work more hours and use up more physical energy that day than most of the others with whom I ate eggs and toast.

Whatever pride I felt lasted through the morning, even though there was not much work to do. This particular project is almost complete. We will soon move to a site somewhere southwest of the city. What remains to be done here is mainly cleaning up. I spent the morning, therefore, raking the dirt on a slope beneath which our sewer lay. It is part of Gus's contract that the land is left clean and level after the pipes are laid. The sun was warm on the slope. I made more of the raking than was necessary, perhaps, but it did fill the time while Gus was away. I was content.

Al, the ex-longshoreman, raked with me most of the time. We talked slowly in time with our rakes. Mainly we talked about work. This is a man who doesn't expect much of his jobs by now. One employer is about like another, one trade like the next. If he gets bad treatment on one job, he moves on to another rather than looking for change where he is. He accepts hard work as his lot and carries his share of the load in whatever he does. It is hard to imagine him letting out a loud noise, either of anger or of joy.

It was a peaceful time for me. Like other shy men, when I am with just one person I act as if the worst thing that could happen would be to let the conversation stop. Keep it going, Jack, or be thought boring or bored. So the words flow on even when they add little of note. Today was different. Al and I talked when we wanted to talk and were silent when there was nothing that had to be said. Neither the talk nor the silence seemed awkward this time.

I had time too to watch the cars that raced by all morning on I-285. Many of the drivers in them were salesmen, I felt sure. I found myself feeling sorry for them and imagining that some of them would surely be happier raking on the slope rather than rushing to make the same sales pitch again. I jump in my thinking from the conceit that no one is quite like me to the bigger conceit that everyone is just like me. This morning I was at that latter point. I was sure I had found a rhythm in my life that men and women in those cars must envy. My job didn't have much status or pay, but it had a sense of immediate utility and also of peace.

The afternoon killed that feeling completely. We did nothing. Almost six hours of nothing. That turned out to be harder than anything I had yet done, even though we were being paid. Back in my job at Haverford, there never was a time without work to do. Sometimes what I did may have been make-work and inefficient, but, when worse came to worst and I wanted to avoid digging into one of the piles of unfinished work on my desk, I could always turn to the latest report from the American Council on Education and persuade myself that I needed to read it—or I could stare out the window in such a way that, if one of my secretaries caught me at it, she would be kind enough to assume I was planning another speech.

But this afternoon there was no escape from doing nothing. Almost everyone except Al and me seemed to be off somewhere doing something. Not us. We stood, first on one foot, then on the other. We tried the north side of the road, then the south. We stood right where Gus, who was in the trailer's office a good part of the time, could see us. Then we got out of his sight. Any small task that Gus gave us came as a relief. We did it with zeal. We even did it over again when that was possible.

Even conversation didn't work as it had in the morning. There's only so much you can say on the subject of boredom before it gets boring in turn. I looked at the cars racing by on I-285 now and thought a salesman's job wouldn't be such a bad deal after all. At least there would always be something to do.

I think it bothered Gus that he couldn't think of anything for us to do at this site. He is never still himself and likes motion all around him. But today he was stumped.

At one point he sent me with the company's mechanic on a one-hour trip on a truck. I was useless on the errand, but I was out of the way.

We had loaded six pipe lengths, a couple of valves, and numerous fittings onto the truck. They were the last loose pieces of sewer or water line left on the site. Our job now was to take them back to the county's water and sewer department to get credit for them. One large water valve had a missing cap, and I learned from the mechanic that the valve was worth about $250 complete but was of little value without the cap. He hoped for our company's sake that the receiving man in the county yard wouldn't notice it until it was too late.

That man spotted it at once. He stood with his hands jammed deep into the pockets of the county's uniform tan coveralls and looked straight at the mechanic.

"We can't take it. It won't pass."

I was impressed that he saw it so fast. My eyes were much slower. I missed seeing the size of the bill that the mechanic drew from his pocket. All I saw was one hand fly out to receive it and the bill go deep into the county's coveralls.

"Well, maybe we can fix it up."

That was the high point of my day.

As I waited for the papers acknowledging receipt of the parts to be filled out, I got talking with a laborer on a similar mission for another sewer company. He appeared to be thirty years of age. My mouth fell open when he told me he used to be in sales work but had shifted to this job three months ago. "I couldn't take the pressure there any more," he said. "I'm happy as hell now." I almost asked him what college he was president of.

We hadn't talked more than a minute or so when he asked me how much money I made. It has been a long time since anyone other than one of my children or the Internal Revenue Service asked me that. I told him. He said he was making $3.75 an hour, a dollar more than I was. He didn't seem pitying or even contemptuous toward me. He just seemed to take it for granted that this was the way labor markets worked. Some people got a good rate, and others got a poor one for doing exactly the same job. It occurred to me that this man knew what some of our labor economics texts still have not learned about the world of work.

"I think my boss will take you on if you want to shift. He needs good men," he told me. As I noted the name of his company, I thought of the kindness of what he did. He had built a bond at once just on the basis of our doing the same work, and he was ready to help me share his good fortune.

Back at the site once again, time inched slowly along. At one point Gus took pity on me and spent fifteen minutes talking with me by the road. He began by describing the tests used to check the completed sewer and water lines. He spoke with such enthusiasm that I found myself caring more about how such lines are checked out than I would have believed likely before. Gus told me that he had once had 100 men working for him, but he gave up the business a few years ago to concentrate on some apartments which he built and still owns. That work bored him as soon as the buildings were up and occupied, so he turned their management over to his wife and reentered the pipelaying business on a more modest basis. His contacts were still good enough and his record strong enough that he could pick up contracts with ease. Today he has work lined up far ahead. I do not know whether he makes much money with so small a crew. From the way he talks, I doubt that it matters much one way or the other. He has an outlet for his energy and that is what counts.

This is a tough, demanding man. What he says wouldn't look too good in the personnel books that I've read. Yet his directness works on this job. And there is so much fairness and competence in him that he earns respect. Neither in today's talk nor in the briefer ones I have had with Gus before did he ask anything about me beyond what he learned that first evening on the telephone. So far as he is concerned, my life is strictly my own affair. He will judge me by how I act on the job.

In the last hour of the day I got a further assignment. Any task at all was a treat by then. In preparation for the move to the next site, the last of the equipment was being stowed away. Gus told me to dismantle and clean the heater that had been used to warm hands on cold days. It was heavily coated with soft soot from the diesel oil that had burned in its belly. There was no way to clean its pipes without getting thoroughly black—face, hair, hands, and clothes. I looked like one of the coal miners from *How Green Was My Valley* as I drove back to the motel—which may explain the looks I got in the supermarket where I stopped to buy groceries for tomorrow's lunch. The motel towels, and a nearby laundromat, removed the black.

I called my oldest son, John, tonight to tell him I'm well. We had agreed I would do so each Wednesday. If the college or one of the other children needs to get in touch with me, that is the link.

Talking to him told me anew how much my current family situation made this form of leave possible for me. If I were still married, I would have needed a very understanding wife. Being divorced is usually no fun, but it has its advantages this spring.

From my children I got what I most needed for the trip, a sense of their believing in me whatever I chose to do. A couple of years ago in a late evening of frivolous talk, I told my daughter Nancy, who was nineteen then, that I thought someday I might like to leave all my credit cards behind and just work my way around the country for a while. It was the closest I came to sharing my plan with anyone. I added no details, for there were none to add. Nancy responded with immediate warmth. "Dad, I think that's great."

I knew she'd understand. This is the kind of

thing she might do herself. She plans very little as she goes along, but things work out just fine for her all the same.

I am much less certain about how John will react to what I am doing. He's well organized, thorough, a natural-born planner-ahead—the kind who has time to press his blue jeans the night before an exam. But he showed an instinctive faith in me by volunteering to look after my checking account and bills, keep an eye on the house, and deflect all queries about my whereabouts.

It was the same with the younger three. Each had his or her own way of saying, "We believe." I think Steve, who is twelve and an ecology nut, is secretly hoping I'm spending the leave at Assateague Island seashore counting egrets and plovers. And tonight I think that could have been a good idea. Even bird-watching must be more interesting than standing around doing nothing at a job site.

Thursday, February 22

Today wasn't much better than yesterday.

It was moving day. We drove to the new site at a housing development south of Atlanta. Gus told me to drive one of the company trucks. He didn't ask me if I had ever driven one before, so I didn't tell him this was a new experience for me. The only instruction I got was to follow the truck in front.

Halfway there, I panicked. Suppose I should lose sight of the other truck in the fast traffic on

I-285? I saw myself going into the state troopers' barracks and explaining my plight.

"Pardon me, officer. I wonder if you could help me get where I'm going."

"Certainly. Where do you want to go?"

"I don't know."

"You don't know?"

"No. You see, I was following one of my company's other trucks down the road and I lost it. We're moving to a new work site south of the city."

"Fine. Just tell me the site and I'll tell you the way."

"I don't know. Nobody told me."

"Well, why don't you call the company's office and find out?"

"I can't."

"Why not?"

"I don't know the company's name."

"Well, then, the best thing for you to do is to go back where you started from and ask someone there to help you out."

"I can't."

"Why not?"

"They've all left. There's nothing there but the pipes underneath the ground."

"Look. You just head for your home with the truck. Park it out front and go inside and lie down. You may have to wait a couple of days, but eventually your boss will call to ask where his truck is."

"He can't. He doesn't know where I live."

I saw the ghastly scene ending with my being sent off to a Georgia chain gang for stealing a truck. Just before they took me away, I'd have to call the Haverford board chairman in New York and say, "John, a funny thing happened on my way through Georgia." Once that thought was in my head, I stayed so close to the truck ahead that other drivers must have thought I was being towed.

When we reached the site of the housing development—the signs told me its name was Pine Hill —there was little work for us to do. In time there might be, but not on this first day.

Al and I spent a couple of hours down in new manholes shoveling out the wet mud that had gathered there from recent storms. The trick of this was to find a way to get full and dripping shovelfuls of mud through the small opening above our heads without spilling most of the dirt back into the hole or onto us. Al was in his manhole, and I was in mine. We had no chance to learn from one another. But without any time pressure on us, there was a chance to experiment alone with various techniques. I never did find a good one, and if Al did he didn't share it with me.

That job done, we were without useful work once again. By now there were five of us to stand around most of the day, criticizing the shoddiness of the materials and workmanship going into the new homes. Men with no work of their own become sharper in their criticism of the work of others. Yet that kind of talk won't fill a whole day. So we discussed the profit possibilities in the two canteen trucks that went by, wondered why the bricklayers on these houses were all black and their laborers were white, contrasted Gus's and Dick's leadership styles, counted piles of pipe lengths several times, and took as long as possible eating our sandwiches at noon.

Then we talked politics. We were a racially mixed group and some of the talk may have been guarded on that account. There wasn't much optimism about politicians in what I heard. "They're getting theirs, just the same as before." Lester Maddox came across as someone both colorful and close to the man in the street in his style; but he didn't seem much different to these men, white or black, in what he finally did or cared about.

There wasn't a radical thought in the crew. These men had jobs, they didn't expect government to make those jobs much better, and they were more concerned about future tax bills than about future public aid. On this one work site at least, the ground is barren for the seeds of change. And the political rhetoric I sometimes hear at home would blow away in the wind.

The boredom of the day got to all of us. I had heard each of these men complain about the heavy work we had done earlier this week. I saw now that that was a different kind of complaint. What I had heard before was as much a boast as a gripe; it was a reminder to ourselves of how much we could do when pushed. Today's moaning was the real thing, a call to be spared from doing nothing. Perhaps it is true, as some writers have said, that the work ethic in America is on the decline. Yet, on the basis of what I have seen on this one job, I cannot agree. These men go on acting as if they want to work when they are at work and to play when they are at play. Just don't mix up the parts of our lives, they ask.

We have a long chance to play in the next few days. From time to time Gus cuts the work week to four days so that there can be time for hunting and fishing from Friday through Sunday. He has just bought a new camper, and the next three days are ideal to try it out. We are off work until Monday.

From our point of view, this is fine. Most of us already have forty-six hours of work on our time cards this week, so we are into overtime now. Gus never promised us more than that. The younger men in the crew in particular are anxious to get off into the woods.

There were paychecks for everyone but me at the day's end. I don't get one until next week. However much I feel part of the crew by now, I need a check in my hand to know that I'm working for pay and not for fun. I know too that I'm running low on cash. Besides, I want a check so that I can learn my company's name at last.

Friday, February 23–Sunday, February 25

Three days off. By now I'm ready to go back to work.

I have been alone for these days. With nobody telling me when to come to work and what to do, I quickly reverted to something like the life I lead at home. Only it was harder here. I needed to watch what I spent, for one thing. Atlanta is a vibrant place, one that I think I would like. Still, its free sights scarcely fill one full day. I went first where I

50

usually go in a new city, to the art museum. The new building was fine, but the collection was thin. Some Samuel Kress money had bought a few magnificent old masters; after that, the galleries had little to show. The public library left me depressed; neither the building nor the books seemed worthy of Atlanta's place in the South. A stroll through the state capitol buildings didn't take long. And watching the ups and downs of the open-shaft elevators on the Regency Hyatt Hotel's inner-court walls soon palled.

Only Underground Atlanta, reconstructed alleys of taverns, cafés, and shops beneath the street, told me of the city's pride in itself and its belief that great cities have places for fun as well as for work. Unfortunately, Underground Atlanta's fun comes dear; my sampling of it, beyond walks past the shops and peeks in the doors, will have to wait until I come back in another role with more money in my pockets.

As I drove around inside the city and out, there was an awareness that wasn't there before. I noticed sewer and water pipes wherever they lay along the roads. In the museum I wondered who had laid its underground pipes. On a drive out to find a state park for a sleep in the sun, I stopped at a construction job along the highway to watch a sewer crew at work. The picture seemed familiar to me, even to the detail of two laborers standing around looking bored. When I jumped a bit at a shouted order from a boss to one of the crew, I knew it was time to get out of there.

Walking through the galleries at the museum, I had felt somewhat out of place. The clothes I wore were about like those I would wear to a gallery at home, yet I felt different—awkward, even—in them, as if I were putting on a show. My hands are blistered, swollen, and cut in places, not like the hands of the other men I saw in the gallery this week. Had there been someone with me from our crew, I could easily have said as I looked at some abstract oils, "Hell, I could have painted those." Back home, I'd have used the sophisticates' reply to that line, "Yes, but you didn't." Tonight I don't know whose side I'm on.

There was time for reading in these days. I brought a boxload of books with me, and they are spread around my room now. Most of them are of the sort I have intended to read on vacations or long winter nights and have never got around to finishing. Writers like James Gould Cozzens and Thomas Mann, books like a biography of Sigmund Freud and the true story of the Light Brigade. I dipped into most of them a bit, just about the way I have done in the past. Then I turned to the same favorites that drew me before—George Orwell, Elizabeth Bishop, Robert Coles. Maybe I could never tell those who share my love for those books why I liked these past days in the ditch so much. Maybe I could never tell the men with whom I now work why I read what I read. That doesn't matter to me. These two parts of a life away from home feel in harmony for me.

What surprises and pleases me is how relaxed I feel about what I am doing and also about what may be going on back home. In just one week the perspective on Haverford begins to get clearer. I'm surer now that Haverford has two core missions by which it must finally be judged: to provide a quality education and to teach its students how to live with their fellow human beings in trust and concern. Everything else the college may choose to attempt must be determined by its relevance to those two goals.

I know that the definitions and books on "quality education" are both long and complex. The heart of the matter for me is simple enough: Are we turning out young men who can think both critically and humanely? It's not our job to see that they know this or that set of facts; the world is far too complicated for us to agree any more on what set of facts any well-educated person should know. The most we can do—and it's a great deal—is to help them separate facts from fiction and keep a healthy respect for both. They shouldn't be thrown for a loss by any new situation in which they find themselves; their skills at solving problems should be ready for use. Likewise, they should never be trapped into thinking that the facts are all that matters; they should also be able to think in disciplined ways about abstract ideas, and morals, and matters of taste.

I don't have many doubts about our ability to meet the highest tests for our education, just so long as we have the courage to take a hard look at ourselves from time to time. What has been worrying me more this week is whether we have the will to make the way we live and work together on campus a central concern once again. If one single thought about my ambitions for the college were to linger on, I know which one I would want it to be. It would be words addressed to students that went something like this: "No matter how sordid or ugly the rest of the world may become, I want each of you to know from your experience here that it doesn't *have* to be that way. I want you to know at first hand that men and women can work together in trust and respect." From the perspective of the ditches in Atlanta, I see how far short we have fallen in building that kind of world on campus. I see how petty and self-pitying we have been on many occasions, how smug and isolated on still others. If the ditches teach me nothing else, they've taught me how incredibly fortunate we are—and how much we owe it to the society which supports us to lift up our eyes and reach for the stars.

The hours when I stood idle this week didn't seem to help me think about those tests for the college and for myself. It was the hours when my muscles were most in play which seemed to give me the time and the desire to get things straight in my head. Gus Reed has bought my arms, legs, back, and a small part of my brain for $2.75 an hour. That's a fair bargain, because he has left the rest of my brain to use as I wish.

I've had a good chance to think back to how I became president at all. It was a more complicated hiring procedure than Gus used. Searching for new college presidents can only be compared with a Victorian courtship. Each party knows very well what the other has in mind, but neither wants to be so crass as to be the first to put intentions into words. On the one side is a committee that pretends to have no problems at all. It acts as if the position at its disposal is so attractive that anyone given half a chance at it will say yes at once. Yet, if the committee is of age, it knows that the market is tight and the list of criteria drawn up for the one to whom the proposal will finally be made fits no one alive. That committee also desperately wants to avoid being turned down. So most of its inquiries are variations on one theme: "We don't say we're asking you to come—but, if we did ask you, would you say yes?" On the other side is a candidate anxious to be asked, a little afraid of being left on the sidelines, but still attractive enough to have a less interesting suitor or two in the wings. So most of his responses are variations on another theme: "I'm really very happy with my life as it is—but just what did you think I could do for you?"

Haverford and I went through a series of ritual moves for quite a while. There were my visits to be looked over by everyone in the family in a general, polite way, then visits to meet the key people in the family at tighter range; there were talks about the future of higher education, then talks about dollars and cents. On the surface we were casual and polite enough, for we both knew the rules of the game. Behind the scenes, we were digging deeply into one another's past.

Since 1833, all the presidents of this undergraduate liberal arts college for men had been Quakers. I was not, nor did I have any past ties with the college. I had been on the campus once but couldn't quite remember how to find it again. There was no obvious reason why I should have been asked. However, presidential material was scarce that year, and I did meet two of the tests for the job. I had enough experience as a professor and not too much as a dean to pass muster with the faculty—and enough experience giving away foundation funds in New York to pass muster with the board. The college's formal proposal came in the fall of 1966. I was asked to become the ninth president of Haverford.

I liked the campus and its people from the first visit. By every test that I knew of, this was a choice place to work. I had just been through a divorce that was painful to me and was willing, even anxious, to make some kind of fresh start away from New York. It seemed likely that I would accept.

I worked for the Ford Foundation at the time, and I went in to see President McGeorge Bundy one evening at 5:00 to tell him that I would take the offer from Haverford the following morning. Mac had been good to me; he had given me wide rein in designing more ambitious programs for the foundation in the area of equal economic and social opportunities for minorities. A program that made perhaps $3 million in grants per year when he first came was well on its way to $20 million in grants just two years later. If Mac liked you and your work, he was an extraordinarily supportive and generous boss to have.

The challenge of what we were trying to do, for blacks in particular, was already big. We both knew that it would be bigger still. I hadn't talked to Mac for more than half an hour that evening before I knew that I couldn't leave Ford. How could a man pull out of the most-talked-about arena of the day, urban minority affairs, and retreat to a suburban ivory tower for men? All this was before the student

56

movement took firm enough roots to push the campus to center stage.

I called the Haverford board that night and said no. But often that winter I found myself staring out of the twelfth-story windows at 477 Madison. More often than not I was staring past the spires of the cathedral across the way and down toward the Main Line of Philadelphia. I was happy in what I was doing and felt we were about to make some exciting grants. But I saw how many of the professionals at Ford and other foundations had grown lazy or arrogant after their first few years on the staff. Few people can handle the experience of being begged to year after year. I didn't trust myself to become one of that mere handful of pros who avoid the trap of thinking that this was their money they were giving away.

Haverford did not find a president that winter. In March 1967, the board's chairman called me at Ford to ask if he could see me the next day. Without a moment's delay, I agreed to talk to him. As soon as I put down the telephone, I knew what I had done. If he was going to give me a second chance, the answer would be yes this time. It was.

I don't pretend to know all my motives for saying yes that March. There is obviously prestige in the job; there is some respect that goes with the title whether I earn it or not. The pay is good—but no better than I made with Ford. There is visibility and a platform from which to say what is on my mind. There is something heady about working with young people and with men and women up through ninety years of age. The academic pace is not nearly so relaxed as outsiders believe it to be, but it is a pace which gives heavy weight to the change of seasons and which is revitalizing on that account. Above all, however, there is the prospect of making a difference this way. A man accepts a presidency when he feels deep inside that he can do some part of the job better than anyone else can. Modesty requires, of course, that he say it was the urge to serve youth which called him to the post. More often it was a private conceit about his own worth that he heard.

Had I known then what I know now about presidencies, my guess is that I would still have taken the job. A friend told me once that holding this job is like being pecked at by a flock of geese. He's right, but it's deeply satisfying work too. As a result, longings to be academic administrators lurk in far more hearts than most people realize. On our campus as on others, if you take a close look at the goose who leads in pecking at the president, you'll find someone quite willing to make the big sacrifice and fill the incumbent's shoes when the cackling is all over.

Monday, February 26

I came to work full of hope that I would be busy. I was.

Gus set me to work with sledgehammer, pick, and crowbar to remove the wooden frames from around the fresh concrete bases of homes to be built in the project. I couldn't figure out what this could possibly have to do with a sewer and water-line company. But never mind. Banging the frames loose from the bases and pulling all the nails out of the lumber, I fancied myself a carpenter—or an un-carpenter, at least.

It doesn't take long to get used to the shifts into this new world. I scarcely give a thought now to the fact that I have no idea what I am going to be asked to do on any day, that I never hear why we are doing what we are doing, and that my opinion is certainly never sought on any matter concerning the job. I come here when I'm told, do what I'm told, eat when I'm told, and go home when I'm told. For the moment, that feels just fine.

The crew does not change much. There are at least three of us—Al, an Asiatic mechanic's helper whose name I still cannot catch, and me—who ap-pear to be somewhat on the fringe in terms of any long-run commitment to the company or the job. But the others whom I see most often give the impres-sion that they will go on in this work for years to come. They are at home in what they do, and they seem to do it well.

A good part of the men's lives on the job is filled by talk of their lives off the job. Anything they choose to share of their private lives immediately be-comes the business of us all. So Stanley's decision to put the money down on a boat tonight is our joint concern. In the past week we've discussed the price back and forth. Some think it's a bargain, some a raw deal. We have all talked about where to keep it, when to use it, and how to preserve its hull. We were all relieved when the mechanic broke down and agreed to fasten the trailer hook to Stanley's car so that the boat can be towed. It will take almost half a year of Stanley's wages to pay for the boat, but the thrill of its speed can be shared by us all.

"Man, that fucker'll take off like a greased shot out of hell. That's one baby I won't be able to hold down."

Now it won't matter so much whether Gus bawls Stanley out or not. He's getting his escape.

I realize how much quieter I am on the job or at lunch here than I am at home. Beyond my usual reserve, I'm anxious to avoid answering too many questions about myself. Actually, no one pushes hard on my past. They know I am from Pennsylvania, and they think I used to be in sales but got tired of that; the readiness with which they accept that motive for taking a laborer's job tells me they would make the same choice themselves. They know too that I am divorced; that has made me something of a ditch lawyer, since one of the younger men is about to go through the same process himself. "There's no such thing as a friendly settlement" has been elevated to the status of Coleman's Law.

But I'm quiet too because I'm not knowledgeable on the two most popular topics for talk: hunting rabbits and hunting women. Those seem to be the only legal game at this time of year in Georgia. If I let my mind wander in the lunchtime talk about one or the other, I get confused when I tune in again as to which game is now being chased.

"I had this one big one lined up so I couldn't miss. I had her before she even knew I was there."

"You should have seen the one that me and my buddy got out near a park. She took one look at us and she knew she was done. It was just a matter of time. Man, she was scared. And she should have been—we were both that hot."

Both types of game are there for man's purposes, it is clear, and both eventually succumb to man's attacks no matter how long or involved the pursuit. The variations on the chase theme are somewhat limited, and one day comes close to exhausting the possibilities. Yet there will be a replay of them the next day in a different order, with new appreciation for the narrator's style.

When the talk turns at lunch to the more public news of the day, the older crew members talk more than the young. What they have to say is said briefly. When a man has points to make, he makes them and gets out of the way. The prolonged refinements and playing for extra points that are so much a part of the talk in my world just don't fit in here.

The three blacks on Gus's crew are an integral part of the work. There's no race line that I can see on competence, assignments, or effort. On the days when all of us eat together, however, I've noticed how often Robert, Langston, and Al sit next to one another just a bit removed from the rest of the group. Even there, the talk flows across race lines in such a way that anyone seeing a transcript of what was said wouldn't know the white speakers from the black.

One thing that all the crew shares is a generous use of four-letter words. I came to this job with the idea that I could use "fuck" and "shit" or not as I chose. That idea died about the second or third day. If I wish to be heard, I have to use them. My accent is somewhat unusual to these men, as theirs is to me. I'm asked to repeat what I said much less often now that I have the right quota of the four-letter words sprinkled throughout whatever I say. They are integral parts of the rhythm of speech, punctuating a thought here and highlighting another one there. They sometimes become oral hyphens, as in "Coca-fuckincola." The real masters of language can use them to separate syllables, as in "Hell, no, it's all the way downtown in Atfuckinlanta."

These are seldom dirty words and are no more often angry ones than they are happy ones. A word like "motherfucker" here is often just a synonym for man, no more and no less. ("Who's that new mother-fucker over there?" or "I told the motherfucker we'd pick up him and his bitch at eight.") No one is going to tell you that you are a good man in this crew. The closest you can come to an open expression of respect is when you are called an obscenity by someone who is smiling at the same time. That's a clear enough message, I suppose.

For one who has gagged over these words before (to the amusement of students), I'm somewhat at home with them now. I find it equally natural to leave them at the work site when I drive off at night.

Tuesday, February 27

At last I know my employer's name. I heard Gus use it in talking to a friend at the site.

"I'm National Utility Corporation now. I gave up that National Plumbing bit."

I rather like the sound of the name. It could look very good on my employment record to say that I was once with National Utility Corporation; it brings to mind images of electric-power magnates and high finance.

I was a carpenter's helper this morning and got to put in nails instead of pulling them out. The job was again on the new home foundations where I had ripped boards away yesterday. The cinder-block walls were high enough now that they needed wooden supports to give them extra strength until the floors were laid in. The carpenter who guided me is one of Gus's crew. He told me that Gus takes on some concrete and foundation work in case there isn't enough pipe work for his crew. That helped me understand both yesterday's and today's chores.

The boards I nailed in place today will eventually go on the scrap heap, but at the morning's end they represented my handiwork. Long after a boy loses his ambition to be a fireman, the yen to be a carpenter and work with wood lingers on. Today I could act out a Walter Mitty–like fantasy for those few hours. I wished my son Paul could see me then. He can do everything with his hands that I can't. Had he caught me at just the right moment, he'd have seen me hammer a nail in straight and he'd have been proud. But I doubt that the carpenter was that much impressed. I feel he must have wondered when he asked me to start laying boards at the right end of one wall and I immediately set off for the left end.

How could he know I still have trouble telling my left from my right, especially when the pressure is on?

It might have helped if I had told him there and then how we almost lost World War II because of my left–right problem.

I had gone in the Canadian Navy as an Ordinary Seaman. (That's what the admiralty called me, but I frankly never felt ordinary.) In a short time, because of my college degree and little else, I was sent to the officers' training school in Halifax. There had been enough corvettes lost in the North Atlantic and enough new ones built that the school decided to speed up the pace of putting new officers through. As a result, two separate classes were graduated on the day that I did.

The officers-to-be who had the highest marks in the three-month course commanded their classes on the final ceremonial day. I had made it to the top of my class by a process of psyching-out tests. A close friend of mine made it to the top of the other class in the same way. We were two proud young men that day.

His class was graduated first. We had carefully rehearsed the ceremony for days before. Some sort of British admiral was to be there for the day, and the school's commander wanted a first-rate show. The ceremony was on what anyone else would have called a field, but we tars called it the deck in traditional style.

I was shocked to see my friend slip up in his role at the very last minute. He was supposed to ask the admiral's permission to lead his class off the deck, but he forgot. I couldn't imagine how. The admiral and the school's top staff looked aghast as he blithely marched them away.

It was my turn now. Everything went as we had rehearsed. When it came time to leave the deck, I used a smarter salute and a louder voice than were really necessary to ask permission to go. The admiral beamed as he said, "Carry on." He knew that he had a quality man in me and that the battle of the North Atlantic might yet be won.

I turned to face the class. I went blank. I couldn't remember whether I wanted them to turn right or left to end up heading the way we were supposed to go. But I had to say something. I blurted out, "In threes, left turn."

Half the class did what I said. The other half did what we had rehearsed with such care; they turned right. There were the members of the class, standing in rows staring at one another cheek to jowl. Titters rolled across the deck through the classes still in training.

The admiral was the first to speak. I heard his precise but disgusted British voice say, "Subleftenant Coleman, will you please take your gang off the field?"

I stuck with the order and marched us off to the left through barriers and mud on the unpaved way. I was damned if I would admit I was wrong. I did resolve, however, to work on that problem of telling left from right at some future time. But I've been busy since then, and the right moment hasn't yet come.

The pride I got from my carpentry this morning was short lived this afternoon. Some older person in loud checked pants and white shirt went by busy-busy-busy at least six times while I was waiting for another job to do.

Gus told me later with a big laugh that the man had asked him, "Who's the old guy who works for you and does nothing but go over and stare at the valves every once in a while?"

Obviously, that man was a horse's ass—first class.

The day ended busily. We went back into a clearing in the woods to lay storm sewer. The pipe for this is about fifteen inches in diameter. But it is aluminum, and a length of it handles easily in comparison with either the clay sanitary sewer pipe or the cast-iron water pipe. So the work moved ahead fast. Gus was in his glory, working the backhoe himself, keeping an eye on absolutely everything, and happily yelling away at us all. No kid with a dump truck for Christmas and a bit of imagination had more fun than Gus was having.

My own job alternated among bringing the pipe to the ditch, putting on the bolted joints linking one length to another, and shoveling dirt onto the completed line. There is a lot to show for even one hour's work with pipe this large.

No part of the job here is more satisfying than the soaking bath afterward. The clothes by the tub are caked with mud, but I come out clean again. And there is a special sense in which I feel that, whatever my dinner later, I have earned the food I eat.

A full day laying more of the storm sewer. This time we were without Gus.

The coverup code for sloppy workmanship is complex here. The tests of whether we are laying a good storm sewer or not are in the slope of the line and the tightness of the joints. There is no faking it in the slope. The county inspectors have the same laser beams we do; all they have to do is shoot the beam through from the bottom of one manhole to the next one to tell if we did our job right. The joints are something else again. Sometimes the pieces fit together easily, and sometimes they never quite mesh. The crew on the line hurries to cover as many of the joints as possible with a thin layer of dirt before the bosses come along; the joints get buried well before we turn to the rest of the pipe. The bosses then order the poorer fits among those still showing to be covered before the inspector comes along. The inspector wants the work to pass the test if he likes the contractor, so he looks to get the last of the pipe buried too.

Whatever we have done is soon out of sight. It just remains to be seen what happens when the first heavy storms come along. I don't know a good storm sewer from a bad one. Yet, by and large, I thought we did honest work today. I can recall one or two joints that I wish I had done better, but I'm not ashamed of my work.

Each day I see more clearly how awkward I am

at most jobs requiring the use of tools or equipment. I didn't drive that truck well (how long has it been since I used a gearshift at all?). I know now that I don't use a sledgehammer, a chain saw, a ratchet wrench, or a pipe cutter very well either. When I was in high school, my ineptness at athletics was well known. "We don't want Coleman on our team" were familiar words to my ears. I half expect to hear them here in reference to my use of tools. Certainly that explains why so many orders to me begin, "John, get a shovel and . . ." That is one tool I use well.

The expectations held out for a laborer are not high, however. Part of the time it is enough that he be there, an impersonal item on hand when needed. A young, arrogant employee of the developer at Pine Hill illustrated that point today. Some mud splattered onto his all-too-clean levis as he stood near the ditch. Noticing it, he reached a hand toward me for my shovel, scraped the mud off, and returned the shovel, never once having looked at or spoken to me. The shovel was there, and that was enough.

Dick, who is normally a decent and warm guy, represented another aspect of this attitude to laborers. He was mad at Stanley, who had forgotten two items when loading the truck back at the trailer today. Gus, being Gus, naturally noticed the mistakes. That brought Dick, as the supervisor for this squad, a dressing down. As he drove me to the job later, Dick said, "What bothers me most is when you rely on a guy like Stanley and he lets you down. He's a pipe man and knows better. If he were just some goddamn laborer, I wouldn't expect anything of him. But he's not."

Just a goddamn laborer. Would I ever get hardened to hearing that if this were my life's work? It is a precondition for loving others that any man love himself first. How can he do that if the part of his life which is his job is treated in so callous a way?

This concern is easy enough for me to feel today because I am just a goddamn laborer for these next weeks. The test is whether I'll feel it when I get back to my regular job. Someday I'll leave Haverford. I'm vain enough that I'll want faculty, students, and board to say at that time that, all things considered, I've done the job well. But it will matter just as much to me to hear men and women in the secretarial posts, housekeeping, buildings, and grounds say that this college treated them with respect.

To the extent that anyone back on the campus feels tonight that he is just a goddamn laborer, we have failed as much as if we cheated him in his pay.

Thursday, March 1

We were still on the storm sewer this morning. This time we went through woods far from the road to a low, swampy place where the line would end and discharge its flow. The mud was thick, wet, and seemingly without bottom.

We were determined to load the truck with all the gear this morning. We know how angry Gus can be when something is forgotten and our work is delayed. So we had shovels, sledgehammers, laser, battery, wires, measuring rod, tape, gasoline-driven saw to cut the pipe lengths, masonry trough, trowels, chain lengths for lifting pipe and manholes, ratchet, wrench, bolts, and wire cutters. The pipes and joining bands were at the site. Perfect.

To be sure, Dick, as the man in charge, checked again. Perfect once more.

We wallowed in mud which was just about as deep as Gus had told me it would be that first day. A shovelful of it made a sucking sound as it pulled away from the ground and thick, black water oozed in to fill the space left behind. It was the kind of mud that boys always hope to find and that their fathers always hope to avoid. But the work still moved along nicely. We came to the last pipe length. It was too long by a few feet. All that had to be done was to start up the saw and make the one cut of the day. We tried it. The engine was out of gas.

That left us with a problem. We had forgotten to bring the gas can. Just then Gus came along. The time required for someone to go back to the trailer to get the gas gave Gus ample time to discourse at length on just how stupid we were. It was quite a colorful talk.

He was down on everybody today. His invective is endless. There are no shadings between what he says when we have made a major error and when we've been just a little bit stupid. Only the length of what he says tells whether it's a big deal or not.

Dick caught its fullest force at the day's end. Under his direction, we moved out of the swamp to bury a twenty-four-inch storm pipe under what would be one of the developer's major roads. It was the biggest pipe I had worked on, and I felt I was in the big league now. We were within half an hour of being finished with the job of laying the pipe and connecting it to the huge pre-cast concrete blocks that marked both edges of the road and the intake and outlet for the drain. We had followed stakes put there by the developer's engineers in placing the headwalls and pipes. Gus then appeared. One look was all he needed to know that we were wrong.

"You're goin' to have the fuckin' headwall in the middle of the fuckin' road. Use your mother-fuckin' head, you shits."

"But, Gus, we're just doing what the stakes said to do."

"I don't give a damn what the stakes say. Look, you can see where the fuckin' road is goin' on this side. And you can see where it's fuckin' well goin' on the other side. How in shit is it goin' to bend around to miss your goddamn headwalls?"

"But the engineers put the stakes . . ."

"Fuck the engineers. It fuckin' well ain't right. Use your goddamn eyes."

That was just the warmup. It was followed by speculation on Dick's parentage and the quality of education given engineers in college these days. This was the longest of his speeches to date. I never found out whether Gus was really right. It hardly mattered, anyway. So far as we were concerned, if Gus said the stakes were wrong, they were wrong.

Dick is a man one has to like. The six of us on his crew were solidly united behind him, not because we were so sure he was right but because he was our man at this point. He was the one who sweated it out while we tried to maneuver that monstrous pipe into place. But our support was of no use to him now. We stood silent and embarrassed until the boss was done.

Gus hadn't really exhausted his theme when he had to stop. A county safety inspector came by and, after looking over the crew, took Gus aside for a chat. When Gus returned, he was a little milder in his tone. But not much.

"Startin' Monday, everyone wears the hard hat I gave you. Every fuckin' one of you. And, Stanley, you either cut that goddamn long hair or you put it up in a net, do you hear?"

Stanley heard. But he didn't like what he heard. "I ain't wearin' no net."

"Suit yourself. It's the net or the hair. I don't give a shit which you choose. We're goin' to be safe. This is a fuckin' hard-hat job, just like I been tellin' you."

We were silent in the back of the truck as we rode back to the trailer tonight. Only Carl, the backhoe operator, could find the right words. He spoke without anger or blame. He simply stated the facts.

"One good thing about Gus," he said, "is that he's always right—even when he's wrong."

Friday, March 2

This was my last day here.

It was to have been the second to the last. I had

72

told Gus earlier that I had to get back to Philadelphia and would be quitting tomorrow. But it rained, a soft, steady rain beginning in late morning, so we were sent home at 1:00—that is, the newer men such as Al and I were sent home, while the veterans were kept busy on make-work jobs for the afternoon. The forecast is for more rain tomorrow. Gus has decided there's no more work this week.

We were laying a twelve-inch clay sewer pipe in a fifteen-foot trench along the main highway. This was not only the deepest trench we had seen; it was also far and away the heaviest pipe I had been asked to lift. It took two of us—and one was Braden, the ex-Marine, so that alone is like having two men there—to lift each length into the bobcat tractor's bucket to get it to the trench. I knew in those morning hours exactly what "straining one's gut out" meant. If ever there was a time to get a hernia, this was it. It helped me to see that Braden was straining too. That was brutal work by any man's test. I'm frankly proud that I did as well as I did.

These were good men to work with. In my days with them, I never saw any of them stand idle while someone else was straining on a job; there are different skill levels and rates of pay, of course, but the men all share in the loads.

Even as I left, Gus was yelling about something in the rain. That seemed the right way to end.

Braden asked me this morning, "Have you ever worked for a swearing fucker like Gus?"

I admitted that I hadn't. I could have added too that I'd do it again.

A free day that I hadn't counted on until yesterday.

The weather was wet enough to prove Gus right again. We couldn't have worked. I have to be in Philadelphia by Monday, but I didn't want to go home yet. It would be too tempting to get caught up in campus affairs if I stayed at my house more than one night. So I drove part of the way home, found another eight-dollar motel, and settled in to read.

Placed somewhere between Atlanta and Haverford, I find my thoughts running easily to contrasts between Gus Reed's leadership style and my own. If someone had told me about Gus before I made that first telephone call two weeks ago, I might never have called him at all. That would have been too bad.

There's not much of his remarkable style I could copy back on the campus even if I wanted to. Suppose I singled out some academic department at a faculty meeting and delivered my thoughts as Gus did. "You're the shittiest bunch of professors I ever saw. You call what you're doing good teaching? Why, I fucking well recall when I handled classes twice the size of yours and still gave every goddamn student more fucking attention than you bastards do. You don't amount to nothing and never will."

After a period of silence, a few of the faculty would say, "Let's talk this matter out." The peacemakers among them would suggest that we refer "the president's concern" to a standing committee.

One or two professors, once they saw that everyone else was shocked, would predictably take the other side and utter words they'd gag over at any other time: "I think the president's right." But most of the faculty would simply agree that it was time to have me committed to the state hospital, which fortunately is only a few blocks away.

No, I couldn't use Gus's style. But it sure would be interesting to try.

Sunday, March 4

Coming onto the campus this afternoon, I realized how much I enjoy being away. The lane is lovely at every time of year; today, winter's colors were still on the trees and the grass by the pond. Those colors have a magic of their own for anyone born in a northern climate. I could enjoy them this time without feeling the responsibility that usually sweeps over me when I drive up that lane. I didn't even notice whether there were stray bits of litter along the road or whether there were strangers on the paths. I didn't wonder what messages would be lying on the hall table for me. That's freedom.

I know how lucky I am to be president here, and I will never be able to give up the job without regret. I can cite more instances of pure joy from the Haverford years than from anything else I have done, and I have had a good life up to now. But this job can beat a man down. There is no way to survive it without a sense of humor; there may also be no way to survive it happily without chucking it every once in a while.

Organization charts show the president of a college on top, just a step below the financial angels. In actuality, a president is at the center of a web of conflicting interest groups, none of which can ever be fully satisfied. He is, by definition, almost always wrong. If he spends much time meeting with students, he is neglecting the faculty. If he spends much time with the faculty, he is being dictated to by them. If he is off campus, he should be back minding the store. If he is on campus, he should be out raising money. If he pushes his pet educational thoughts, he is trying to run the show. If he doesn't, he is not interested enough in education. If he changes his mind on an issue, he is wishy-washy. If he doesn't, he is pigheaded. If his name isn't in the paper, he is letting the school down. If it is, he is a publicity hound. If he smiles a lot, he is naïve on the problems of the school. If he frowns, he has given up too soon. It's all very interesting, and not hard to take once he gets over wanting to be right and settles instead for doing the best he can.

That is the most a man or woman can do, for the demands go on and on. In 1972, for example, we had a major confrontation on campus on black–white issues. Those were the most intense days of my presidency to date. The pressures and counterpressures mounted as talk became blunter and nerves more taut. The climax for me came in an all-night negotiating session with black and Puerto Rican students to work out the text of the college's commitment to more diversity in its student body, faculty, and way of life. We had a deadline to meet the next day, and the entire campus knew it. We completed the agreement in my living room just before dawn. The students went home to bed. Two hours later the administrators were at their desks beginning to figure out what the commitment meant and preparing to brief all segments of the college on what was up. I had a difficult but encouraging meeting with key members of the board of trustees from 3:00 to 5:00 that afternoon. There were loose ends to tie up after that. It was 7:00 in the evening when I was alone at last. I felt I had played a part in steering the college through tough days, but I have never felt more drained than I did when the last person left my house.

Just then the telephone rang. A young faculty member told me that the college and I were mishandling a fringe benefit matter. Ordinarily I'm too proud to admit to fatigue, but not that night. "Please. I'm very tired. Can't it wait?"

"No. It will just take a few minutes. But you've got to correct your mistake."

"Look. I just finished twenty-four solid hours of meetings with only one hour of sleep. We've reached an agreement."

"I'm glad it worked out. So, now let me explain my concern. . . ."

As long as it is that part of the job I remember in the quiet of the night, it is too soon to come home. In time, all the bigger satisfactions will come back to mind.

Two

The time of my quitting in Atlanta was dictated
by a meeting in Philadelphia this morning. I became chairman of the Board of Directors of the
Federal Reserve Bank of Philadelphia on January 1.
Even though I had a leave from my college job, it
hardly seemed fair to ask for one from the bank post
where I had presided over only four meetings so far.

Each of the twelve regional banks that make up
the Federal Reserve System in the country has
nine directors—three bankers elected by the member
banks in the district, three business leaders chosen
by the banks, and three public representatives chosen
by the Governors of the Reserve System in Washington, D.C. I have been on the board for two years as
one of those public members. We have the same
general responsibility for the oversight of the Philadelphia bank's affairs that directors might have in a

private concern. Washington can veto our choices for top officers to operate the bank, but usually the voices of the local directors dominate in choosing the key staff. We review general policy issues with the local officers through a number of directors' committees. We exercise an audit function over the bank's assets and operations. By law, we are the only one who can initiate recommendations for changes in the lending rates which the Reserve Bank charges to those private banks that borrow from us.

The directors meet at least twice a month. I had asked the Deputy Chairman, a Philadelphia corporation officer, to preside over some of the directors' meetings during my leave from Haverford. But one matter required my presence today. This was the day when the examiners from the Federal Reserve System in Washington were to make a report to the Chairman on their review of the bank's affairs for the previous year.

The year 1972 had been a difficult one at the Philadelphia Reserve Bank. There had been a major theft—it was usually referred to as a "defalcation," but from my dictionary I knew it was just plain stealing. Over $1,000,000 in currency which was slated to be destroyed had been filtered out of the bank in an incredibly complex plot. The employees involved in the scheme were arrested and ultimately convicted, but effects on morale of a theft from within the bank spread in all directions. Scarcely anyone close to the units which count currency and those which destroy tired old bills could be automatically cleared of suspicion. Investigations by the FBI and lie-detector tests became a part of the bank's life for some weeks. This one theft meant that every one of the elaborate security precautions had to be gone over again. Indeed, there was a danger for a while that, under Washington's prodding, we might become so security-conscious in order to preserve the bank's good name that we would forget we also had critical ongoing services to maintain. For example, we process over three million checks a day for the banks, firms, and individuals we serve. A few delays there and the costs would be as great as any involved in the theft.

I thought of that background as I went to the meeting this morning with the Washington examiners. We had new officers in our top positions on the bank's staff, and, though we felt they had done extraordinarily well in coping with the morale problems, I wondered if Washington would see it in the same way. "Examiners from Washington" has an ominous ring to it. A man can seem calm on the surface in going to receive their report; underneath, he can be as nervous as the first day he reports for work on a sewer line and wonders what is in store for him.

My special problem in going to the meeting was that I had to pinch myself in order to remember what role I was playing this time. Was I really a bank director? Or a college president playing a bank director? Or a ditchdigger playing a college president playing a bank director?

The bank itself seemed unreal when I went into it. I knew from a receipt I signed when I first took over the chairmanship two months ago that I was technically the custodian of more than $4,600,000,000 in assets. I had never been to the vault or to the account books to verify the existence of those assets. I just took it on faith that they were there. No wonder the place seemed unreal. The Atlanta ditch was a novel place for me to find myself at this age, I admit, but so is a post where numbers like that are treated so casually.

The Federal Reserve Bank in Philadelphia has an austere front. Its white marble and heavily guarded doors tell the passersby that this is a nononsense spot. I was aware of a switch in roles as soon as I went into the building through the Chestnut Street door. The guard greeted me with "Good morning, Dr. Coleman." That's not the way they said hello at the construction trailer. It was the same wherever I went in the bank. Yet I didn't feel myself a better person on account of the title or politeness today. I know that I still have to prove myself at the bank as I had to do in Atlanta. I'll have made it here when I'm called Dr. Coleman with the same smile that I was called an obscenity on the pipeline.

I met with the examiners in a second-floor office, the kind of uninspired office that says "Be comfortable, but be dull." We were alone. These two men had met with many board chairmen before; by law, there is regular turnover in our posts. So I was once again the new boy. They showed deference to me by virtue of my post; with it, they showed skepticism by virtue of my newness in that post. One of their questions carried both tones at once: "Dr. Coleman, what else would you like to know?"

What I learned about the bank for 1972 was generally favorable. There were few surprises in what I heard. But I had a different attitude toward the session than I might have had a few weeks ago. I was struck most by how roundabout our sentences were and how little we communicated to one another in simple, unambiguous ways. Whatever I learned beyond a few surface impressions was more often in well-guarded response to my questions than as a result of the examiners' independent offerings. Their test for me, I suppose, was to see whether I knew the right questions to ask. Both the examiners and I wore clothes that were in style for men in our positions; that is, nothing we wore was memorable. We matched our talk to our clothes. When they had something critical to say, they did so in such a circuitous way that I probably missed much of it, and I replied in kind. Whatever happened, I learned that ditch English has a power to communicate that bank English lacks.

When we had finished talking, we thanked one another politely and exchanged hopes for a good year ahead. I stopped in at the bank president's office on my way out of the building, but I had little to tell him that he didn't already know. As I said good-bye to him he inquired about my leave.

"Where did you get that tan?" he asked.

"Out in the sun," I replied. That was like the other answers of the day.

My car was in the parking lot a block away. I put the examiners' report in the trunk, took off my jacket and tie, and put on an old sweater. Just before I paid the charge and pulled out of the lot, I went to a pushcart across the street to buy a pretzel with mustard. I consider that food from the Philadelphia streetcorners a treat, especially the mustard part.

But I can't yet bring myself to buy one when I have my business clothes on.

I headed north for Boston and made it here by midnight.

Tuesday, March 6

I came here confidently.

This was familiar territory. I had my first teaching job here at M.I.T. from 1949 to 1955. I had moonlighted during those same years at both Tufts College and Brandeis University, making an M.I.T. salary that had started at $3,900 a year go a little further. I learned much about the area through living in three of the suburbs, Winthrop, Woburn, and Stow. I had visited many of the union halls in the course of doing a series of interviews with steelworkers on their attitudes toward their union. Three of my children were born here, in 1949, 1951, and 1953. I bought my first home here from an old woman whose sole eccentricities were a love for retired horses and a kindness to people; she sold us the house in Stow for a down payment consisting of every dollar we owned, all twenty-five of them. Boston was in my blood.

Coming here yesterday was a sentimental act rather than a rational one. I came without knowing anything about the local labor market in 1973. But I thought that any man who had landed a job on his first try in an unknown city like Atlanta would have little trouble in a known one like Boston.

There was bad news from the start. I was dressed and ready to begin the search by 6:00. It was almost 7:00 by the time I found the morning papers. There was not one ad in either of them for outdoor labor. Was Boston closed for the winter? Two of the temporary labor agencies were beckoning with "Cash paid daily. Report at 5:30 A.M.," but their assignments were as likely to be in warehouses as they were to be outdoors. I felt sure I could get better pay than they offered, and I wasn't ready yet to go sit on one of their benches and wait to be sold as part of a package of four or six or whatever. By the end of the day, I am no longer so sure I will be able to avoid selling myself that way.

At 7:30, I started to use the telephone. I changed one dollar into dimes at a coffee shop and used the telephone just outside. That dollar gone, I changed another one into dimes. Working from the yellow pages, I called construction companies and lumber yards. I tried two moving firms, with lilting Irish names, and some window-washing firms. There was no encouragement anywhere. "Try us again in a few weeks" was as close as I came to a job.

Still confident, I switched fields. I decided to try restaurant work. I may be awkward with construction tools, but I can make out in a kitchen. When my wife and I separated in early 1966 after twenty-three years of marriage, I was aggrieved and miserable, angry at myself for being an inattentive husband. Our youngest son, Steve, was five at the time. On the day when I finally agreed to leave the Tarrytown house which we had bought three months before and to move into Manhattan alone, Steve put a note in my hand. It had obviously taken him a long time to write it, but the words were all correct: "Dear Dad: I hope we see you again." Not even that note could lift my spirits. But I made one resolve that day: No matter what else happened, I was going to learn to cook a decent meal, and I was going to sit down to such a meal every night even if no one else was around. I kept the resolve. I learned to cook—Craig Claiborne's *New York Times* book was a crutch for a novice with ambitions to be a gourmet. I got over my bitterness about the same time that I learned to put a whole meal together. That was the time when my children started to enjoy coming to see me again. I didn't stop to figure out why; I just went on exploring new ways with food.

The more I learned about cooking the better I liked it. Maybe this was because my mother was such a good cook (the main thing I recalled from watching her work was to measure everything carefully and then throw in some more). Maybe it was because her father had been a mining-camp cook for some years, or maybe it was simply because cooking is such a creative art for those of us who can't draw. I knew I wouldn't qualify for anything but a menial job in a restaurant, but I saw myself learning by watching the cooks out of the corner of my eye, even as I cleaned vegetables or washed pots.

There were only two ads. I followed up on the first. It turned out to be ARA–Slater, the same company that caters for us in the Haverford College cafeteria. Wouldn't the executives I knew in that company be surprised if they learned I had been on their staff? The job was in a cafeteria in a shed of the Navy Yard in South Boston. All three—cafeteria, shed, and yard—were gray. I took one look at the faces of the staff (even the blacks looked gray in that light) and left without talking to anyone. There would be better jobs, I felt sure.

The second ad was for a nursing home. I didn't think I'd learn much about cooking there because I already know how to make Jell-O. So I put that one aside, while noting the telephone number in case nothing else turned up.

I tried direct visits to some of the well-known restaurants, places like Durgin Park, Jimmy's in South Boston, and even the Parker House. I don't think I went into a single one of them without walking past the door several times first. I knew I didn't have much to lose, but I still had to screw up my courage every time before I opened the door to go in. Once in, I forced a smile that was big enough to be friendly but not so big as to be foolish. I usually got friendly smiles in return until I stated my business. Then the manner was suddenly haughty. They looked me up and down as if measuring me for a dishwasher's uniform and concluding I wouldn't fit in one. People who have jobs are masters at establishing their advantage over those who don't. Not a person gave me any encouragement about a job except for one man I talked to at Durgin Park. He was as friendly to me as I had heard the restaurant was to its clientele. He assured me there was always room for another good man to join in the bustle there. It turned out that he had nothing at all to do with the hiring. When I did find the right man, he was even colder than those elsewhere. I was impressed at the ease with which he put on a smile for new customers coming in and took it off at once to resume his rejection of me. Not a trace of his daily quota of cheer went to waste.

There were still the regular employment agencies. I steered clear of the State Employment Service because I thought their interviewers would be veterans at their work and would trip me up on the answers I fabricated on the application forms. But I decided that a fee paid to one of the private firms would be worth it if I landed the right job. I tried to tell from the yellow pages which agencies handled restaurant work. Two seemed most likely.

I went first to Thompson's Agency on Tremont Street. The office was big enough for two persons to work in and for applicants to fill out forms in. The man in charge seemed interested in my story about wanting to get out of sales and into cooking. (Strange in a market-oriented society how readily people understand a desire to turn away from sales!) He said he liked my willingness to start at any kitchen job at all in order to break into the field. But he had only one job on hand, and it too was in a nursing home. I said I would think about it and left.

The other agency, Revere, around the corner, seemed even less promising. That office was big enough for just one man. He was busy filling out income-tax returns for clients when I came in. That didn't augur too well for the volume of placements he made. He too masked his surprise that someone my age would be ready to start at the bottom in the restaurant field; he said it was "interesting." By this time, I had filled out the same basic application form a number of times. I did it again here, wondering all the while how long these pieces of paper would lie around Boston files. (An enterprising reporter from *The Boston Globe* went around to the Revere Agency after the story of my leave got into the press three months later. He asked for my application and found that the agent had written across its corner the word "*meshugene.*" In Yiddish that's a little stronger than "crazy.")

The agent had an opening. It was at Stuart's Restaurant in South Boston, a short walk away.

"The job is heavy and fast. It's a porter–dish-washer, but you'll learn sandwich-making and meat cookery if you keep your eyes open. I'm not sure the boss will take you, however. He may feel you're over-qualified."

That was a word I had heard before—from Haverford alumni who had lost their jobs and tried to get back onto the work ladder a rung or two be-low where they had been pushed off. I still hoped nothing would rule me out on the bottom rung. With a week's pay committed to the agency, I hurried over to Stuart's. It was 1:00 by now.

The cafeteria stood alone in blocks of ware-houselike buildings. Its rough red brick front was the cheeriest sight in three blocks, a pleasant contrast to the dirty windows of the adding-machine com-pany up above. I was discouraged and hungry by now. But Stuart's seemed friendly and altogether hopeful. The captain's chairs were filled with what I decided were truck drivers and warehouse clerks. The plastic plants along the wall were free of dust, and the floors and tables were clean.

The serving counter at the back of the room was busy. The customers called out their orders to the four sandwich men under the counter lights and got their selections in rapid-fire order. I stepped up to the first man back of the counter on the left end; he looked busier than the others but he also had a knowing air.

"What'll you have?" he asked even while he cut the corned beef for the man ahead of me in line.

"The boss, please."

He shot a sharp glance at me. "What do you want him for?"

"I'm from the employment agency. I want a job."

He didn't miss a stroke in his carving but spoke in Italian to an older woman nearby. She beckoned me to follow her into the kitchen behind.

We passed through the kitchen, which looked spotlessly clean. These people obviously weren't sitting waiting for the new porter–dishwasher to come on the job. In a back room off to the left of the kitchen, she unlocked a closet door and, with a combination of Italian and gestures around her own waist, she asked me the size of my pants.

I mumbled, "Thirty-four."

"Ah, trentaquattro," she replied. I thought we were doing fine. But I noticed that the white pants she handed me were size thirty-eight. The thought flashed through my head that I was expected to eat a lot. I felt lucky I had worn a belt on my regular pants.

She gave me a white shirt with "Stuart's" embroidered on it in green and an apron. Then she indicated a corner of this small room in among the tomato juice and pickle cans where I was to change. There was also a large pair of rubber boots where she pointed. I couldn't tell whether I was to put them on or not, but I decided to wait to find out.

I remembered the agent's words of caution and told her that I thought the boss probably wanted to interview me before he hired me. She didn't understand but caught the word "boss." She then led me back to the same man at the serving counter. He was as busy as before.

"What do you want?" he asked sharply, again with scarcely a glance at me.

"I thought you'd want to talk to me about whether I got the job."

"Didn't you come to work?"

"Yes, but . . ."

"All right. Work." He turned his attention to pastrami.

I went back to the storeroom to change my clothes. I put on the uniform and came into the kitchen. No one acknowledged my presence. I looked stupid and begging for a while. That didn't work, so I stepped over to a man loading the dishwashing machine.

"Hello, I'm John. I think I'm supposed to wash dishes."

"I'm Ed. Ever done this before?"

"Not really."

Ed was about my age, but had a sallow face that had seen little sunshine in its life. He was my height, six feet or so, equally thin, and his shoulders seemed to sag more than mine. He looked at me with tired eyes through steel-rimmed glasses and smiled just a trace of a smile.

"You'll learn. We'll bus dishes first. Come with me."

He chose a two-tiered cart that stood by the sink and led me back into the dining room. "Watch me closely."

He meant just that. There was a precise place reserved on that cart for each size of plate, glass, and bowl.

"You don't have to do it this way, but I find it helps."

It turned out that I did have to do it that way. I made an early mistake and placed a salad bowl on a pile of soup bowls on the cart. Ed made the correction with an audible groan. He had met my type before; still, he was friendly enough to me.

"Don't knock yourself out. It's quiet now."

We bused dishes for half an hour or so. By then there were no dirty dishes left anywhere in the dining room. I had carted away the empty beer bottles from every table to the dim bar in the room next door; we had wiped all the tables, some of them twice; and I was eyeing the few customers who still had plates before them to see when their last bites were gone.

The cart was finally full. We returned to the kitchen. Loading the dishwashing machine behind the stoves was a well-planned routine. Every dirty dish had but one way to go in. Just when I thought I was getting the knack of loading a tray of dirty sandwich plates, I'd find out from Ed that there was a way of getting four more such plates in the tray. I adopted his method and even tried to fit in a fifth extra plate. He took it out to wait for the next tray.

"You don't have to do it this way, but I find it helps."

I must have sent fifteen trays through the machine and filled one garbage can with slops. The woman who had given me my uniform watched from time to time, neither approving nor disapproving. Ed told me she was some relative of the boss. One meat cook in the kitchen smiled at me in that half hour. Others passed close by but didn't act as if I were there. I assumed they had seen dishwashers come and go before today.

It was five minutes to two when Ed and I returned to the dining room.

"We mop the floor now, half at a time. This is five minutes early, but that's all right. Start piling the chairs on the table—like this. You don't have to do it this way, but . . ."

"I'm sure it helps."

I had just begun when the boss came over to me from behind the counter. "What's your name?"

"John."

"I'm afraid you won't do. This isn't your work, I can tell." He put two dollars in my hand.

"But why?"

"It's not your work. Sorry." He was gone.

I changed my clothes and was out on the street within five minutes.

Fired! The first time in over thirty years of holding jobs. And I still don't know why.

I was in a mild state of shock and anger as I

walked back over the bridge to the center of the city. I looked at people I passed and wondered if they knew what it was like to be thrown out on the street.

I was a more humble man when I walked in Thompson's Employment Agency again and said I'd be willing to take that nursing-home job after all.

"Sorry, you're too late. It's gone. But keep in touch in case anything else turns up."

I tried a few more restaurants that afternoon. By now my morale was low and I suspect it showed. I just couldn't muster up the same enthusiasm when I walked into each new place. Whatever my actual words were, I suspect that they came out sounding like, "I don't suppose you have a place for me, do you?"

The man at Thompson's Agency had told me it was a very slow time in Boston. "We have seven percent unemployment when the rest of the country has five. And we have more young kids here than any other city. That's a statistical fact. We're carpeted wall to wall with kids. They're all after the same jobs you are. It's tough."

This day hit me hard. I have a secure, or reasonably secure, job to go back to. My family's bills are being paid while I'm away. I can still use my name to open doors here and there. But none of that mattered today. I felt unwanted and out of work. I wondered why people couldn't see what a valued employee I would be. I have heard people say I have charm. Why didn't it work today?

I blamed the market and the employers in the morning. The economists in Washington had messed up part of the scene; the local companies had done the rest. Certainly the fault was not in me. By night I felt differently. From the moment I was fired from a job that I knew to be vacant, I turned the blame on myself. For the first time, I began to understand what men and women of my age who lost their jobs went through.

The Haverford alumni who lost their jobs as a result of canceled contracts or the like started out confident that there would be other choices open to them: "Actually, it's probably good for me. I was going stale there anyway." But many times they found no one rushing to hire them. Their self-esteem fell each day. By the time that they were willing to settle for a little less than they had had in income and rank, they lacked the show of confidence necessary to land on that rung. The next jobs offered them, if any, were still lower on the ladder. That took another period of time to accept. The downward spiral for those off the ladder was fast and cruel. Its effect was on their faces, in their speech, and most of all in their walks.

Here, in a space of one day, I felt some of that happening to me. Yet I know it shouldn't be that way, since I was only acting. Get ahold of yourself, man.

The fact remains that I have to do better tomorrow. There are other ways for me to get money, but nothing short of a job will boost my morale any more. I can't even sing tonight. For me that's bad.

When it was too late to find any jobs today, I started to think about the night. I still have enough confidence that something will turn up that I read the rooming-house ads. One of them brought me to the Kenmore Square area, where I applied for a room.

The young man at the heavily locked door asked, "Are you employed?"

That was salt on my wounds. "No," I said, "but I have a chance. And I have cash to pay for the rent."

That was enough for him. He let me in.

The building might have seen fine days. There was enough outside decoration around some of the windows, over the arched doorway, and in the weathervane atop outlined against the sky to hint at a former elegance. The dirt from the years now left everything a uniform gray—stones, woodwork, and window glass. The only variety in the seven floors of the exterior was in the state of disrepair of the dark green shades in each room. The lobby too had hints of an elegant past, but most of those hints were covered by a host of crudely lettered notices giving the rules of the house.

The young man gave me two further pages of rules to read before he showed me a room. Most of them had to do with the rent. The rest were restrictions on appliances, guests, noise, and trash.

We passed a few of the tenants on our way to look at a second-floor room at the back. They were either very young couples, the men all with beards and the women all with ponchos, or much older men by themselves. To get to a room that was empty, we wound through a corridor with enough left and right turns to frighten me at once about fire. Each door on the hall was a different color, the choice of the last tenant there. The one we finally came to at the end of the maze was adorned with a large sticker proclaiming "LOVE."

The room was high ceilinged, paper curtained, dirty windowed, and unadorned. Around the edge of the worn linoleum and along the gray-green walls were a cheap bureau, a sagging couch propped up on two-by-fours, a small desk and chair, a table with a hotplate and a wooden box of dishes, two cots whose drooping springs were poorly hidden by the faded green spreads, and a shiny new refrigerator that was waist high. The bathroom, long and thin, had vintage fixtures all in a row.

I looked at two other rooms, neither of which had a bath, and came back to this one. The rate was twenty-seven dollars a week for a minimum of three weeks. I took it, partly in the faith that I would find a job, partly in a mood of despair. I knew I wouldn't do anything about the torn green shades on the windows or the two naked forty-watt bulbs high over my head, but I thought that a couple of posters, a desk lamp that I would buy, and my books scattered around would make it a livable place.

The car presented a problem. The man at the door told me there were garages and backyard spaces for rent nearby, but the prices were high. After some driving around, I found a large lot some blocks away where for $25 I could leave the car for a month. I hoped I wouldn't have to use it in that time and could close it out of my mind until it was time to leave Boston again.

I now had a place to stay. I could put an address on any employment applications I filled out from now on. I desperately hoped I wouldn't have to do that more than once. Time is wasting, and my mood is low.

Wednesday, March 7

The same rounds. The same results.

I started with the same two employment agencies at 9:00. Neither had a single kitchen job today. But the agent at Revere said, "Try again at eleven. That's when they come in."

The morning *Globe* had two ads for countermen, and one for cafeteria help from a familiar address in Cambridge. It was an electronics plant on the bank of the Charles River, two doors from where I had worked as an assistant professor at M.I.T. twenty years ago. I took the subway to Kendall Square in Cambridge and hurried along the back street to the plant. Each step of the way I expected to meet one of the faculty members I still knew in the Sloan Building. I knew that if I did they would want to discuss economics—but not the kind on my mind.

The lobby at the plant was guarded and institutionally bleak. Another applicant and I were told to wait awhile. Then we were led by the guard down a long hall. I caught a glimpse of the cafeteria on the way. Shedlike and colorless, it reminded me of the one at the Navy Yard. It was almost deserted in midmorning, and the few employees in sight were moving at a slow pace. One seemed to be dusting cornflake boxes. It was that kind of day.

We were shown into a cramped office, where the manager, Mr. Buttrick, acknowledged our presence by pushing two blank pieces of paper our way.

"Go in the room next door. Put down your name, address, social security number, last two jobs, and reasons for leaving."

That was all. I wrote quickly and returned the sheet. He read it without a change of expression. I thought I ought to say something, so I told him I wanted to learn cafeteria work from scratch. He wrote "Willing to train" across the top of the page and told me they would call me Friday after all the interviews were over.

"I don't have a phone." (He hadn't asked for my number anyway.)

"We'll send you a telegram."

"Couldn't I call you?"

"Not really because . . ."

"I'd really like the job."

"All right. Call us Friday."

"Perhaps Thursday?"

"That's early, but . . . all right."

There was no enthusiasm in the way he spoke, either about my chances or about anything else. This one might work out, but I'm not optimistic tonight.

I took the subway back across the Charles and headed for the two places advertising for countermen. One was so dirty that I passed it by. The other was a shiny new place on City Hall Plaza. The young manager there was as friendly as Mr. Buttrick at the electronics plant had been cold. But he wanted more experienced help. He said there might be a place for me in "the back room" within a couple of weeks. I would start on dishes but he would move me into cooking as fast as he could. Now what would I do for two weeks?

I headed back to the Revere Agency at 11:00. This time the agent didn't even have income-tax returns on which to work. But he did have one job open. It was for a porter for Union News in North Station.

"I was sort of hoping to get something in food."

"Oh, they've got a lunch counter there. Maybe two. It's not the best, but it's a place to start. Of course, that's not the main part of the job. Mostly it's stocking the newsstands. You ought to give it a try. Go over there and ask for Molly. Tell her you want to be in food."

I went over to the station. A student writing his thesis on the decline of passenger traffic on the rails in America could scarcely find a better place to begin his research than in that building. Everything about the place suggested that the last train had left a few days ago. I looked for the lunch counter. It seemed to sell tuna-fish sandwiches and chocolate bars, and not many of those. I knew then that I would spend the day stocking the stands with *Popular Mechanics,* paperbacks, and cough drops. Moreover, I would have to cart cigars around; every man draws the line somewhere, and I draw it there. I called the agency back: "No, thanks."

My options now were few. There was still that nursing home which had been advertising in the *Globe* for kitchen help for two days. It was time to try that now. A telephone call confirmed that there was still one job open. I was told to come out at once. The home had a fine rustic name, and that augured well, I thought.

The ride out to the Dorchester section of Boston, by streetcar and then bus, was long. A steady drizzle was falling, and the air was biting cold. This was Boston at its springtime worst.

The bus driver told me that he stopped right at the door of the home. I kept looking for sweeping grounds and a stone lodge at the end of a poplar-lined lane. But he stopped at something far less imposing. It was a small two-story red-brick building close to a crowded street, the type that seems to have been put up without any help or hindrance from an architect. The patients' windows facing the street were dirty and wet, but one could still see the signs of death and decay through their panes. Drooping plants, empty Coke cups, and dusty get-well cards were on the sills.

The lobby was small and dimly lit by cold lights, but it was not dark enough to hide the sight of the very old people filling all the available seats. Their bodies were thin and sagging like the chairs on which they sat. The color was gone from their skins. But, most of all, the life was gone from their eyes. They looked, but they didn't seem to see or care. Nothing in the room relieved the gloom. Eight people on eight chairs waiting for eight ends.

A porter told me there would be no one available to interview me for a couple of hours. I said I would be back, but I knew I wouldn't be. I learned in just that brief moment that I wouldn't have the internal strength to work in this next-to-the-last resting place. These lost faces would haunt me even if I were confined to the kitchen for the entire working day.

The bus back to town was slow in coming. I stood in the drizzle, my back to the home. A part of me said, "Jack, go back and make a try for that job. That's part of life too." Another part of me said, "You haven't the courage to try." That second part won out, and I got on the bus when it came without ever looking back at the home. I hoped someone stronger and kinder than I am would take the job, but maybe it would be somebody who simply needed a job, any job at all. I felt ashamed of myself, but I made no move to get off that bus and go back. Color me yellow.

The drizzle continued throughout the afternoon. A few more telephone calls and a few more spot visits to coffee shops and cafeterias produced nothing at all. I wore a face to match the day.

I decided to try a different agency, Miller's Employment. It was high above the street in a carpeted office that was a distinct improvement over the other two which I had tried. The agent, Mr. Klein, had an immediate prospect and said that he might have another possibility by tomorrow afternoon if the first didn't work out. The job at hand was as a dishwasher at a country club in a suburb to the west; I recognized its name and imagined that one or more of our alumni might well belong to it.

Mr. Klein was careful not to oversell the job. "It's a live-in job with odd hours. Lots of overtime, you might say. They want you to live in so that you're on the scene. It's not that easy to get dish men out there."

"Will I have a chance to work into cooking?"

"Maybe in time. But don't count on that. If they hire you, it's to do dishes and pots. Maybe prepare vegetables. Don't have any false ideas about it."

He had already referred another man to the job. That struck me as odd, but I wasn't in a position to quarrel. A telephone call to the club told the manager there that I too would be out for an interview the next morning and the club could then choose between the two of us. When he put down the phone, I asked him what my chances were.

"The other man has more experience than you. But then you handle yourself well. It will be a personality matter in the end."

My interview is at 9:30 tomorrow morning. The other man's is at 9:00. Tonight I'm trying to figure out what kind of personality a dishwasher is supposed to have. I know from reading George Orwell's *Down and Out in Paris and London* that a dishwasher (*plongeur*) in the French restaurants of the 1930s was not supposed to have a moustache; that was putting on airs. But I can't remember whether he said anything about personality, and I haven't brought my copy along. I think I'll just try to be grateful and mild.

The dinner I cooked on the single burner of the hot plate in my room added no cheer to the day. There wasn't much to season the ground beef with, and the peas were cold by the time the meat was warm. And you just can't make a very interesting salad out of a single cucumber and a hard-boiled egg. Mayonnaise would have helped. The fuse for the circuits at our end of the second-floor hall blew while I was eating, but that didn't matter too much: There is a brilliant fluorescent light in the alley just outside my windows. Its white glare threw sharp shadows from the fire escape onto the linoleum floor. I could see every bite that I ate.

While I was writing tonight, feeling hopeful about tomorrow but also sorry for myself, I had the portable radio on. Not one station was playing music that suited my mood. But then, in a quick trip across the FM dial, I heard the first bars of the orchestra and tenor in Mahler's *Das Lied von der Erde*. It is that music more than any other that I am likely to put on at home on the evenings when I am low and want to be lifted not by gay songs but by music of an overwhelmingly lonely yet strangely exultant mood. A music programmer somewhere knew what I most needed to hear. The music had never seemed so intense. Some of the words—*"Der Herbst in meinem Herze währt zu lange"* ("The autumn in my heart lasts too long")—hit close to home.

Thursday, March 8

I took a streetcar and a taxi—extravagance—to the country club. Nevertheless, I was late. The day was wet, but the clubhouse looked spotless even in the gray light. The brass fixtures on the front door were well polished, but they were being polished again. On the table in the lounge inside the door, the *Christian Science Monitors, Wall Street Journals,* and *Atlantics* were arranged in rigid rows.

The receptionist was most friendly. Because of the heavy rain outside I had my coat collar buttoned high. She couldn't tell that I wasn't wearing a shirt and tie. As soon as I said I was from the agency, she became appropriately cool. She pointed the way to the manager's office and turned to more important matters on the switchboard.

A man whom I assumed to be the other applicant was sitting thumbing a magazine outside the manager's door. I looked at his face for personality hints. There were none. I was going to be on my own this time.

However much in the dark I am about a dishwasher's personality, I have no doubt in my mind what a country club manager in the Boston area should be like. The manager here was just right for the part. Immaculately pressed dark suit, white shirt and plain dark tie, shiny dome, and metal-framed spectacles—it was all correct. Had stiff paper collars still been in vogue anywhere, he'd have had one on. He seldom changed expression. When a hint of a smile did come to his lips, I felt he had committed an indiscretion.

He had talked with me for only a few minutes when he asked me to step outside while he conversed with the head of the club's membership committee, who had just come in. Their voices were loud enough for me to learn that some club member was living too high and not paying his bills. A third person was agreed upon as the right man to speak to him. That taken care of, the manager turned to me again.

He took me to the kitchen. The chef had been called away after his talk with the other applicant, and I was told to wait. I did so for forty minutes. There was little to interest the eye in a kitchen that was old and scrubbed clean. A woman making coffee told me things were bustling here "every time we have a party." It was hard to see what happened the rest of the time. It was now less than an hour before lunchtime, and this woman, a baker making pies, and two men messing around in a dim corner with pots and pans represented the only life. Still, it was a rotten day outside and this was March. Those are surely bad conditions for sizing up a country club.

The chef came in at last. He looked to be no more than thirty-five. His handshake was warm and his smile the same. He asked very little about my past. That wasn't what was on his mind.

"Are you really willing to work a split shift? It's eleven to two, and five to eleven for you each day—longer when we have parties. You can read or listen to the radio or sleep in between, but those are the hours. Most men won't take them."

I was noncommittal and asked about the work.

"It's vegetables and pots. I'll show you." He pointed to the two men in the far corner. "That's where you'll be most of the time. I'm letting one of those guys go. Alcohol."

I thought about long hours in a sterile kitchen in the service of people with whom I had little in common. I'm not the country club type, and their world seems even farther from mine than the world of the pipeline workers in Atlanta was. I thought about living in this club; the rent I'd lose on the room in Boston bothered me less than the thought of being stuck in this stuffy and starchy place. I suppose we don't differ so much from one another in this world on the question of whether we are snobs or not; the differences are probably on what we are snobs about. I was one today, and my hesitation showed.

"I guess you don't really want it," the chef said. "I don't blame you."

He then did an unusual thing. He had learned I was from Philadelphia. He gave me the names of two chef friends who live there in case I ever wanted to try kitchen work back home.

As I went out the main door, the other applicant raised his head and smiled. I hoped he would get the job.

My spirits on the ride back into town were lower than before. I had only two leads left. One was the industrial cafeteria in Cambridge. The other was the vague possibility mentioned at Miller's Employment yesterday. If both failed, my choices were two: I would either have to quit Boston in defeat, or go to the part-time labor-by-the-day agencies at last. The fact that I had put down so much rent on the room made the day-labor option the more likely one.

On the streetcar, I started to read the ads again and realized I almost knew them by heart. So I turned to other pages in the wet *Globe*. In boredom and frustration, I read my horoscope for the day.

Those born under the sign of Cancer were told to "Look for money and luck in the early afternoon."

As soon as the car arrived downtown, I telephoned the cafeteria.

"I'm sorry. We've hired two other men. But we're keeping your name on file."

Damn the horoscope.

I went over to Miller's Employment. Mr. Klein was on the phone as I walked in.

"I'll be with you in a minute, John. I've got something for you."

Praise the horoscope.

I was amazed that he knew my name. And I was delighted when I heard what he had for me.

"The sandwich and salad man at the Union Oyster House was hospitalized yesterday. They don't know how serious it is, but he'll be out from two to six weeks. If you filled in for him that would give you just the chance you want."

I knew the name at once. The Oyster House on Stuart Street is old; it opened in 1826, seven years before Haverford College began. It was one of those quality places I had heard people talk about when I lived in the Boston area twenty years ago. Mr. Klein added that it paid union rates and was considered a choice place to work.

It was nearby, a few doors from Faneuil Hall and facing onto the City Hall Plaza. The manager and part owner, Joseph Milano, Jr., was near the desk at the front door. His greeting was direct and pleasant. Young, intense, and open, he came across at once as a person I thought I would respect. Mr.

Klein had told me he was considered able; that's the way he looked to me.

The interview was short. He spent more time assuring me that, if I proved competent, there would be a place for me at the Oyster House after the sick man returned than he did asking about any qualifications I might have for the present job.

"I'll pay you the union rate of two dollars and seventy-five cents. I have to. When Lonnie comes back, I'll try you as steward in the dish area at the same rate. I need a man there in charge of that crew. As a minimum there'll be an opening as a dishwasher at two dollars and forty cents. If you're good, we'll find some way to keep you."

He explained that I would need the chef's approval. We went upstairs, through one of the larger dining rooms there, and out into the kitchen. The chef too was young. John Lambert appeared to be about thirty-five, intense, energetic, outgoing, and alert. There was something about him that spoke at once of skill in his art. I decided that I wanted to work for him.

"John's references check out," Joey told the chef. He had to have made that up on the spot.

I was hired. "You can start right away." In the lives of thousands and thousands of people, my three days of "unemployment" would be nothing at all. Yet the relief I felt when I heard those words was real enough to me. My confidence flowed back almost at once. I was determined to do the job well.

Joey took me upstairs into one of the old lofts that crown this nest of buildings. The narrow stairs were steep, the lights dim. The wood of the attic floors and of the sloping beams was dry and slivery. From the way Joey fumbled with the keys as he unlocked the wire-mesh door of a storeroom, I decided that he didn't often escort new employees up here. There seemed to be nothing in the storeroom but uniforms and a few dusty plastic carolers left over from Christmastime. I couldn't figure out why anyone would want to steal from that room; this business too would have its mysteries, I saw.

He gave me a white shirt (now I would have "YE OLDE OYSTER HOUSE" embroidered across the left breast in bright red), white pants, and apron, and showed me where to change. It was a replay of the scene at Stuart's Restaurant, but this time I felt a courtesy that told me I had a chance of making it here.

It was 2:00 when I came down into the kitchen. Now I had time to get a better look at the room than I had when I was concentrating on getting hired. The first words that came to my mind to describe it were "compact and clean." By the rush hour this evening, "crowded" seemed a more apt work than "compact."

Two wide openings at one end of the room led into two pantries, one for ice and ice cream, the other for butter and rolls, coleslaw, and hot and cold drinks. The pantries in turn led into the large dining rooms beyond. As I came through one of the pantries into the kitchen, I faced a long serving counter which divided the room into two. Through its aluminum shelves with their piles of light-brown dishes, I could see the battery of ranges, tall and black.

On my right in front of the counter were the dish-washing machines, the counters where dishes were sorted and scraped, and barrels of trash. On my left there were first a low freezer, then a large double-doored refrigerator and a rack of shelves, and beyond that, jutting out at an angle into the room, the sandwich and salad bar. Nothing in the room looked very new. Everything looked as if it belonged.

There wasn't much happening now that the lunch hour was almost past. The air was heavy with the smell of fried fish, and a few racks were still filled with dirty dishes. But the picture in the bright but cold light from the fluorescent tubes overhead was one of an ordered calm. I was aware that I was being eyed by the cooks back of the serving counter and by the dishwashers off to my right. Once again, no one spoke even to say hello.

The chef came out from the work area back of the ranges and took me to my work station. The sandwich and salad bar was no more than six feet across and about that same height. It had two pass-through aluminum shelves up above, a long, well-worn cutting board and rows of aluminum supply trays at the level of my waist, and built-in refrigerator space down below. To my right were the shelves that stood next to the big refrigerator; they were full of salad bowls and bread above and salad supplies below. To my left, at an angle and no more than five feet away, were the cooks' long counters and stoves.

The chef told me that my name might be a problem. He was John, so was one of the cooks, and so was one of the oyster shuckers downstairs. Too many Johns will spoil any broth. The thought that surnames might be used to tell one of us from another didn't occur to him or to me. They have no place in work like this. I said I'd be happy to be "Jack." That was an easy transition, because I'm Jack at home too.

Tonight I simply cannot recall what else the chef told me in those first minutes. The orders came in so soon afterward that I no longer know what he told me and what I learned for myself. I dimly recall his saying something like, "There's your mayonnaise for the sandwiches, and your bread . . . use these plates for the regular sandwiches, and these for the clubs . . . here's your lobster, crab, and shrimp . . . two pickle slices on each plate . . . your chips are over there beside you . . . don't let the waitresses touch your Roquefort dressing; they can help themselves to the other kinds, but they use too much of the cheese, so you serve it yourself . . . your ham and chicken are out behind." But my memory is hazy. The only clear impression I have is that he seemed calm, trusting, and available. He was the kind of supervisor I'd like to be. Whatever he said, the message still came across as "Go ahead and learn the job—and call for help when you need it."

There is a striking parallel between that and the way I was introduced into the role of teacher at M.I.T. twenty-four years ago. No one said to me then that there was any special technique to teaching a class, even with some of the nation's brightest students. I was told what textbook had been ordered for the course, where my students were to meet, and when I should be there. Someone less shy than I might have asked, "But what do I do the first day?" I didn't ask, and in the years since then no new instructor has ever asked me that question. For the rest, the message from the M.I.T. colleagues who were soon to become close friends was, "When you need help, call us." I thought before today that there must be no other jobs where there is so little training of the novice as in higher education.

The key to survival in both situations may be the courage and sense to ask for help. I know I made mistakes in my first year at M.I.T. because I was too proud to ask for help. And the profession of college teacher is one where none of your peers sees you at work; your classroom is your castle and no one in a position to help would dare to come in. That fact almost ruined my career as an academic administrator in my first hours on the job. Just after my appointment as Dean of Humanities and Social Sciences was announced at Carnegie-Mellon University, I called together the faculty with whom I had already worked six years. I naïvely said that I hoped to visit professors in their classrooms to get a better idea of what went on. There were shock and disbelief. It was as if I had said I wanted them to bring in their diplomas for me to check out. I managed to get into only three or four classrooms, and two of those were the classes of men who had recently won teaching awards. The rest of the doors were shut.

Today was different on that score. Every cook could see what I did. So could the chef, and the waitresses whose orders I was filling. The cook closest to me, Dana, didn't seem to miss a thing I did.

But he responded in such a supportive way that I felt no embarrassment about asking him what to do.

"Dana, I just got an order for a shrimp cocktail. What do I do?"

"Dana, what goes in the club sandwich?"

"Dana, where are the hard-boiled eggs?"

"Dana, how do I get this toaster to work?"

The orders tapered off soon. That gave me more time to look around. I explored the refrigerated space below. The cans of pickles, olives, and tuna made sense. But what were the canned strawberries for?

A waitress called out, "Ordering a strawberry shortcake." To my surprise I saw she was standing looking at me.

"Dana, what do I do now?"

"Didn't the chef say you look after desserts too?"

"No."

"Well, you do."

I found a tray of shortcake in still another refrigerator back behind. Then, as if I had been doing it for years, I produced the can of strawberries from below my work counter. I think I half expected applause. The waitress only said, "Don't bother with the whipped cream. We do that ourselves. You'll catch on. It just takes time."

The key lesson I learned was that this was a kitchen where the orders to the cooks and salad man were oral ones. I had peeked into other restaurant kitchens and had seen the waiters' and waitresses' orders clipped onto wheels or stuck on spindles in front of the cooks. It was those glimpses into kitchens that gave me the nerve to lie at the employment agency and say that I had had two weeks' experience in restaurant work. I assumed that I would work with the written word and that I could deal with the slips of paper in just about the same way I deal with the mountains of paper crossing my desk in the Haverford presidency—quickly if they interest me, slowly if they bore me. But in the Oyster House the written word is apparently a private matter between the customer and the waitress.

What we get in the kitchen is a shout, always preceded by the word "Ordering . . ." I knew at once that this would take some getting used to. It was only in the ditches in Atlanta that anyone had shouted any order at all at me in recent years. And the only time in my life when I can recall someone giving me several orders within the same minute was when I first went into the Canadian Navy and the petty officers in gunnery school made their permanent mark on me by staccato barks of "In *left* threes . . . *right* threes . . . ab*out* turn . . . *left* flank . . . *right* flank . . . *port* arms . . . *shoul*der arms . . ." I hear those barks still.

In the Oyster House kitchen, the orders begin almost as soon as the waitresses come into the room. The older the waitress, the sooner she starts her cry. The words seldom seem directed to anyone in particular. The trick is for each cook and the salad man to pick out those words that apply to his station. So, for example, a call of "Ordering butterfly shrimps, a fried trout, a full order of steamers on the shore, and a lobster salad" sends four men into action at once. The deep-fry cook starts to work on the shrimps, the regular fry cook on the trout, the broiler and steam cook on the clams, and I on the salad bowl. That is, we each start on our part of the order if we aren't doing something else at the time. If we are filling some other order, we just tuck this new one into the next vacant slot in our mind.

I am too confused by it all tonight to describe it clearly. What I see now that I'm back in my room is a fast-moving pattern of the whites that all of us wear against a background of aluminum and brown. What I smell is fish and the sea. What I hear is "Ordering . . ." with a prolonged first syllable and a nasal tone. But what I feel is simply relief. It's the relief of finding a new job, one I expect to like.

The rain had stopped when I crossed the City Hall Plaza on the way to the subway at 10:00. By day, the plaza had seemed rather dull, a desperate attempt by a team of architects to make a center city be talked about. By night—a night when I had a job—it was an intoxicating place. Pools of rain reflected the low lights on each of the plaza's many steps. The rhythm of four steps here, eight there, and twelve somewhere else was exciting; the eye wanted to be everywhere at once. Sharp angles on the steps caught strong shadows. The air was clear. There were few people around. I was tired, but I sang as I walked.

Friday, March 9

My hours are 11:30 A.M. to 9:30 P.M. on Sundays, Mondays, Tuesdays, and Thursdays. Fridays

I stay until 10:00, and Saturdays until 10:30. I'm off on Wednesdays. That makes for about a sixty-one-hour week, or fifty-five if the hours for my own lunch are taken out. There is overtime pay, of course.

I was lucky I started when I did yesterday. Coming in at 2:00 meant I could learn some part of the job while the action was slow. Today I got my first taste of what the lunch hour is like. It is wild.

The first order for a tuna-fish salad came just as I entered the kitchen, tying my apron on as I walked. I hopped to the order at once; Dana had coached me on that one last night. I assumed that as soon as I got it out of the way I could turn to getting my supplies ready for the day. I knew I needed more ripe olives, more chicken-salad mix, and more small shrimp. I knew too that I needed to learn where to cook some bacon; it hadn't seemed right to take it home to fry on the hot plate in my room. But now I wished I had. Hard on the heels of the first order came another, and another. Soon the stream of waitresses into the kitchen was almost an unbroken one. I was trying to catch the orders meant for me even while I drank in the scene. The waitresses crisscrossing the tiled and slippery floor barely missed one another, but not one of them dropped a loaded tray. "Ordering . . ." "Ordering . . ." "Ordering . . ." The room throbbed with their shouts. It seemed as if all of Boston were out to lunch at the same time, and all had converged on the same place.

By now, most of the sandwich orders seemed easy enough. It was just like making lunch for my children over and over again. I don't know why it never occurred to me before when I ordered a sandwich in a restaurant that someone actually made it. By hand. But now I know. A quick slap of mayonnaise on the two slices of bread, a generous application of the filler, a piece of lettuce, a quick closing and a diagonal slice with the big knife, a garnishing of the plate with chips and pickles, and *voilà!* The order was done.

Most of the sandwich orders called for lobster, crab, or tuna. But there were orders too for bacon, lettuce, and tomato, sliced chicken, chicken salad, turkey, ham, shrimp, and egg salad. With three choices of bread, an option of toasted or plain, and varying amounts of mayonnaise each time, the possibilities seemed without end. I tried to affect a casual air as I worked, but anyone who watched me surely knew I had never made more than six sandwiches at a time in my life before this.

The club sandwiches proved tougher to make. There is no special trick to piling a slice of toast with mayonnaise, pieces of chicken, lettuce, another slice of toast with mayonnaise on both sides, bacon, tomato, more lettuce, and a last piece of toast with mayonnaise on top of one another. The trick is to cut the pile neatly once it is done and to get it onto the customer's plate in such a way that he doesn't say to the waitress, "I didn't order a toast salad." Sure, the plastic toothpicks helped to keep it all in place. But it was still a challenge to me so long as a host of other orders were ringing in my head.

The salad bowls offered a better chance to make food look good. Each had a bed of lettuce leaves, a filler of chopped salad greens, the appropriate mound of lobster, crab, tuna, or chicken, and then a circle of garnishes: two each of hard-boiled-egg quarters, ripe olives, cherry tomatoes, cucumber slices, and pickles. Crowning each bowl were slices of Bermuda onion. They looked good enough to my amateur eye that I wanted to admire them for a while before they were whisked away. There was no time for that. I did wish, however, that the waitresses wouldn't nibble away at the choicest bite as they headed back to the dining room with my art.

But the time-consuming part of my job was the chef's salad. I thought that with the first order for one the chef might step over and give me some special secret to set his salad apart from that of all other men in the trade. No such luck. There was no secret—just work. Once the lettuce leaves and filler were in place, I was told to prepare a layer of thin, long strips of ham, turkey, and cheese. Then came the same circle of garnishes as on the other bowls. That extra cutting for the strips was what took the time. Without exception, it seemed that I ran out of some ingredient just when I needed it most. That meant a trip far back of the hot ranges, across the slippery tiled floor, and into the walk-in cooler to find, say, the ham. By the time I got back to my station, another order or two had floated through the air uncaught.

I found that I simply could not keep the orders in my head. An order given three minutes earlier for a crabmeat sandwich on toasted rye and a chicken-salad sandwich on white had a fifty–fifty chance of coming out the other way around. There was one waitress in particular, Hulda, whose orders I mixed up every time. She was young and calm and never bawled me out. But each time I saw her come near I'd resolve to get her order straight just that one time. The harder I tried, the surer it was that I'd be wrong. It was easier once I concluded that she had me marked down for an idiot; I found it possible to concentrate on the other orders then.

But I decided at last that I had to start writing things down. At first I tried scribbling a code on a napkin hidden from the waitresses' view. They saw it and laughed. So I kept the list openly throughout the rest of the lunch hour. At one point my decoded notes told me that I had the following backlog of work:

2 crabmeat sandwiches, 1 on toast
1 child's tuna-fish sandwich
1 chicken salad
1 turkey club sandwich with cucumbers in place of tomatoes
1 chef's salad, extra mayonnaise on the side
1 strawberry shortcake
2 toasted bacon, lettuce, and tomato sandwiches, 1 on whole wheat

I wondered whether the chef's decision not to introduce me into the job in an organized, "here's-what-you-do" way was a conscious one. Or was it just that he was too busy elsewhere to care? My guess is that it was the former and that experience told him the job had too many little details to make a thorough training program effective in the first days.

Yet, if he never gave me a list of things to do, he also never forgot I was there. Several times when it was obvious that I was falling behind, he stepped in quietly, with no fuss or lecture, to give me a hand. I didn't feel put down in any way. But I didn't feel useful then either; there was no way both of us could work in the small space back of the salad bar. Dana, the cook nearest to me at the ranges, was a constant source of answers and of hope. He always acted as if I might make out as a salad man in time.

Today the chef and Dana, with Joey watching close by, taught me about portion controls. I learned that the scale on the right-hand corner of my cutting board had a purpose after all. Yesterday I served the food with a rather free hand. Now I discovered that the crab, shrimp, and lobster must be weighed out each time. Crabmeat and shrimp-salad sandwiches got two and a half ounces of seafood, lobster got two. Crab and lobster cocktails got three ounces. Shrimp cocktail got two large and three small shrimps—their pattern on the plate was also rigidly prescribed. The deluxe cocktails got twice that much, with some extra lettuce too to lift them a bit. The king-size lobster plate got one ounce of meat more than the regular plate. I took a look at the menu to see how much that extra ounce cost the customer: two dollars. Two summers ago, I persuaded a young lobsterman working out of Round Pond, Maine, to take me with him for a day of pulling and baiting his traps; on a clear July morning, he had a good life, but on a cold March morning like today I can't help but think he's at the wrong end of the lobster trade!

I had one order today for a "cheese sandwich, hold the lettuce and mayonnaise." That made the order into a slice of American cheese between two slices of commercial bakery white bread. I looked that up on the menu too. It was eighty-five cents. That made me feel better about the fact that I had put three pickle slices on the plate instead of the regulation two.

With that order, I first became curious to see who the customer was. I knew now that this would be one of the drawbacks of kitchen work as compared with dining-room work: I would never see who ordered what. The customers were in a different world from me, as I was from them. If I identified the appetite for the order with the waitress who placed it, the customer probably identified the preparation of that same order with the waitress who brought it. Certainly, the man or woman who ordered that cheese sandwich wasn't about to send me a message through the waitress, "My compliments to the chef!"

The afternoon was quiet. Not many people ate in the Oyster House from 2:00 until 5:00. Maybe there were guests downstairs at the oyster bar where Daniel Webster, among other big names, used to sit many years ago. But few of them came to the second floor. That left us time to talk and to wait for the evening rush. The dinner hour gathered speed more gradually than the lunch hour had. Instead of moving from calm to frenzy in just a few minutes, the kitchen took on life bit by bit from 5:30 on. By 6:30, all was frenzy again.

From then on the people flow in, the food flows out, in unbroken streams. The rhythm of the kitchen is that of a fast-moving ballet. Small waitresses move in and out among the more buxom ones, their trays bobbing up and down to avoid a clash in mid-air. The dishwashers weave back and forth across the floor to carry piles of plates and bowls from their machines to the serving stands. The busboys dart in and out, their red jackets set off against the light and cold colors of the rest of the scene. And the chef is everywhere—at the ranges, out on the floor, back and forth from the storerooms behind—always the *premier danseur* in search of a partner with whom to star.

I wanted time to watch the show, but there was none. The only person I saw who could do that was the assistant manager, who appeared from below now and then. He stood off to one side playing with his heavy ring of keys, without a trace of a smile on his face. The heavy moustache which pulled the corners of his mouth down toward the floor told of the gravity with which he filled his role. If he enjoyed the ballet, he didn't let on.

I thought of that altogether puzzling incident in the Gospel of Luke where Jesus went into the home of a woman named Martha to teach. Martha's sister, Mary, seated herself at the master's feet to hear all that he taught; we don't know whether she smiled or not. But Martha rushed around and did all the chores that went with entertaining so many guests in her home. Naturally, Martha got a bit upset about this and asked Jesus why Mary shouldn't lend a hand too. Jesus had a curt reply: "Martha, Martha, you are fretting and fussing about so many things; only one thing is necessary. The part that Mary has chosen is best; and it shall not be taken away from her." I have never understood the moral of that story. All I knew tonight was that I identified with Martha a lot more than with Mary.

Saturday, March 10

Whatever the hours are supposed to be, I still made a twelve-hour day of it. I came in a half hour early to get my supplies in order before the noon rush began, and it was 11:00 before I had finally cleaned up my work area for the night.

I enjoyed the whole day. The pace was hectic for a while, and I made errors enough in keeping up with it. But I also worked faster and more efficiently than two days ago. There may not be a formal training course in that kitchen, but learning takes place just the same.

By now, the kitchen's hierarchy has become clearer to me.

At the top is the chef. He wears white coat and trousers and the distinguishing badge of his office, a gold-colored kerchief around his neck. (Actually it's one of the napkins from the dining room, but its effect is equal to that of a small ermine mantle.) He is anywhere and everywhere in the kitchen. He arrives before I do in the morning, to make sauces and soups and to see what supplies must be brought in. He prepares the chef's specials, with help on the more menial tasks from whatever dishwasher is on hand. (His baked stuffed fillet of sole has a tantalizing odor; I'd love to taste it someday.) He disappears for a few hours in midafternoon, then returns to preside over the heaviest of the evening rush. He works long, hard, and fast, but, lucky man, he doesn't have to clean up any utensils or pots as he works. He has his own dressing room with shower up in the loft, just like the Broadway stars. He doesn't punch the time clock like the rest of us. For his lunches he prepares delectable bits of this and that. His word is law in the kitchen, at least until Joey Milano, the owner–manager, appears. Yet Joey too treats him with great respect. Joey knows that a chef is half artist and half manager, and one just doesn't get in the path of artists at work. I sense that if the chef asked for a star on his dressing-room door, one would appear there the next day with no questions asked.

Under the chef come the three or four cooks who are on duty in the kitchen at rush times. There is another cook in a smaller kitchen downstairs, preparing food for the small dining room through which most customers enter the Oyster House from Stuart Street; and sometimes there is a noontime cook in the "1826 Room," a cocktail lounge and the newest addition to this sprawling place. The cooks all wear white jackets and pants, with aprons. Two of them, Bill and Jacob, wear white hats as well, but those hats do not seem to carry special status with them. (I think they cover bald heads instead.)

Each cook has his own station—on the deep frying, the baking and top-of-the-range frying, the broiling, and the steaming. All of them have been here eight years or more. All the cooks are black, while the chef is white. All give an immediate impression of men who know their job, are unflappable under pressure, and move easily in what they do. They share a dressing room upstairs too. And they cook themselves something special for lunch rather than eating the dish listed for employees each day. So far as I can see, none of them likes fish.

Next come the two $2.75-an-hour men, a weekend helper and me. Then the dishwashers, of whom there are three or four each day at $2.40 an hour. Our shirts alone proclaim our employer's name; our aprons, particularly those of the dishwashers, proclaim that we get messy in his service. We go to lunch when the chef or cooks tell us to, and we eat the employees' menu, which is more often beef stew or baked beans than it is fish.

The dishwashers, all of them white, are ignored by everyone except when the supply of some dish is low. There is little conversation between them and the cooks, and none between them and the waitresses. Their work piles up staggeringly high at peak periods when slop-and-dish-filled trays are brought in as fast as the two busboys (why not "busmen"?) can make the trip from one of the four dining rooms to the kitchen. If there is glamour about preparing and serving good food, there is none about cleaning up the mess afterward. Sorting out the garbage in the dish trays is bad enough; worse must be scrubbing the unending pile of pots and pans back in the corner. There the dirt, the steam, the scalding hot water, the poor light, and the bend of their backs must tell them that they are at the bottom. Moreover, if they are old and at the bottom, the chances are strong that they'll stay there.

The kitchen staff is a world unto itself. The waitresses and busboys are in and out of the kitchen all the time, but theirs is a different society. Any authority which the chef has over them appears to be the result of his star status on the premises and not of any formal line of command. They get their assignments from the hostess in the dining room. (Someday I'm coming back here to eat just to see if I can get the hostess to smile when I come in off the street.)

Joey Milano is in and out of the kitchen often. His colorful and well-cut shirts and suits send out signals of his presence at once. He keeps an eye on all that we do, but he is courteous in the way he calls us to task.

He saw today that I was mixing celery and mayonnaise into the lobster and crabmeat sandwich fillings. "I know it tastes better that way," he said, "but that's not the way we do it here. The Oyster House sandwiches have always been just plain lobster or crab. Lots of people have been coming here for many years—and that's the way they expect to find things."

Fair enough. They will be coming here longer than I will, and that's the way they'll find their sandwiches from now on.

I realized tonight as I watched Joey at work that I was watching with envy. Somewhere inside of me there has been a recent but hidden ambition to own a restaurant. I'm smart enough to know that I probably idealize the work and that there are at least as many headaches there as anywhere else. But there is still something about any restaurant with a distinctive flair—this one, for example—that makes me wonder if I'm in the right trade. I wonder if Joey would like to switch jobs.

Perhaps it's my age, perhaps the job I now hold, but I often ask myself nowadays why I'm doing what I do. Why am I in academics rather than, say, doing what Joey does? The answer is far from clear.

There must have been luck and chance on the way. But the first step for me was determined by my father. I cannot recall that there was ever a time when my parents discussed with me or my brother whether we would go to college. The question as I remember it was only, "*Which* college?"

Dad was himself a college-educated engineer, and in his youth something of a rebel in a proud old Toronto family. He broke out of a conservative Church of England home, where for some family members the American Revolution was still a recent and painful insurgence. On graduation he went north to work for a smelting company in what the rest of the family thought of as the wilds. It was to be a short stay, the family assumed, and then he would come back to Toronto's more genteel way. He never left Copper Cliff until, on retirement day, he had to give up the company-owned house where we lived so long. He married the youngest of the four Lawson girls in Copper Cliff in 1915. Their father was at that time a laborer in the same smelter where Dad was a young engineer on the rise. Their mother kept a boarding house only a few hundred feet from the gates of the smelter where acrid sulfur fumes poured into the sky each day. Dad came courting at the boarding house at some small penalty: My grandmother borrowed the coats of any men who came calling to put over the rising dough for tomorrow's bread. So at evening's end Dad would have to brush the flour from his coat before returning to the single men's rooming house where he stayed. But the romance survived.

Dad's attitudes toward college were clear. He assumed his sons would be among the very few in town who got such an education. Except for a mild preference that I become a mathematician (and a fulfilled hope that my brother become an engineer), he didn't care much what we studied so long as it was at one of only three universities which he recognized as strong: Toronto, Queen's, or possibly McGill. Mother was more ambivalent. She was at least as intelligent as Dad. I measured intelligence in those days by skill at crossword puzzles and bridge, and she was an expert at both. But there had never been a thought of her going beyond high school. She may have felt pride that her sons and, for a while, her daughter went away to college; yet that pride was mixed with some questioning about whether it was all worthwhile. She knew so many people in town who were as smart as the few college graduates that she never assumed there was any positive connection among diplomas, intellect, and worth. She was quite mystified about why I eventually went on to graduate school, especially when I had no clear career in mind. "You'll be going to school all your life," she said, and so far she has turned out to be right.

There must be other students who went through their undergraduate years with less exposure to formal education than I got at the University of Toronto, but surely there aren't many. That was my fault. This was a university of the front rank in the world. The riches were there for those ready to enjoy them. I loved each of my four years there. But that love was based on life in the dorms, a career in campus politics, and the first chance for a small-town boy to widen his circle of friends. My major was in political science and economics. After a nervous, conformist freshman year, I attended less than half the classes in every course I took. There was an exception, English. With a teacher like Kathleen Coburn, a Coleridge scholar whose extraordinary skills in the classroom made me want to meet the demands she made on her students, I came alive in the classroom. The rest of my college career was extracurricular.

Graduating from college in 1943 meant that I didn't have to think about what to do next. The war took care of that. But in thinking beyond those immediate years, I usually focused on law. Sometimes, however, I toyed with the idea of studying more about the only subject outside of English that I had truly enjoyed at the University of Toronto, labor economics. The professor wasn't exciting and his materials weren't the best, but he reached me as no one else did and persuaded me that the ways by which people earn their living could be a lively subject to study.

I had one particularly close friend in the Navy. We had as much time as we needed to talk about what would happen to us after the war. First as ordinary seamen, and then as officers putting in time on North Atlantic escort duty, we shared pipe dreams that took us far away from anything we had known before. Russ Best, a city boy, was going to be a dairy farmer; I, less enamored of work, was going to be a lighthouse keeper. Lights like those at Mull of Galloway, Mull of Kintyre, and Donaghadee set me to dreaming each time we brought a convoy through the Irish Sea. That was many years ago. Russ found his dairy farm after short, unsuccessful careers selling marmalade and business forms. I tell him I haven't found my lighthouse yet, but he tells me Haverford may be it.

I was married before the war's end to a fellow student who came from Chicago to the University of Toronto. Mary was great fun, a good student in fine arts, and a lovely, dark girl with brown, soulful eyes. The courtship was short, but the love lasted rather long. Her father was on the faculty at the University of Chicago, and that fact more than anything else led me to Chicago after the war. His field was the Old Testament and he knew little about economics; he told me there were courses in labor economics at Chicago and that proved enough for me to decide to apply. Once I enrolled, I began for the first time to take academics seriously. I had flirted with intellectual ideas at a distance in Toronto; now I had to make up for lost time in a world where disciplined thought was the stock-in-trade. I was thrilled by the university, by ideas

133

themselves, by my special field, and by life with my wife. Soon there was no career I was considering except the academic one.

That puzzles me now, because the decision to aim for a college teaching career came just when professors fell off the pedestal I had built for them. As an undergraduate I knew few of my instructors at all, and none of them well. The occasional Sunday teas in dark, Victorian living rooms were much too stiff to let friendships start; I don't know whether it was the students or the teachers who sighed the most when those teas were done. The teachers and their wives all sheltered me from any hint of faculty politics or strife. I believed, therefore, that professors were models of rationality in all that they did; reason and decorum ruled their lives. Chicago shook me up. My father-in-law, who was about as close to sainthood as men are allowed to come, told me first about faculty fights. Then, through my own teachers, I began to see that the men and women whom I admired so much—and still do—were entirely different once they got into faculty meetings or into dealings with the university administration. Those were the last years of Robert Hutchins's stormy presidency at Chicago. That may have accounted for some of the fighting that went on, but not much of it. The rest was a product of the fact that, however much college teachers love progress, reason, and light within their own fields, collectively they are most often conservative, jealous, and scared. They are staunch friends of change for the rest of the world; but, knowing that there must always be the unchanging alongside the changing, they are quite happy to have their own ways of doing things stay the same. I still decided that I wanted to be one of them.

I have seldom regretted the choice. It is true that I have wanted to sample some other careers, like Joey Milano's, along the way. But most often I come back to my love for the academic life. I still don't know any pleasure to match the one of seeing a student come alive with the thrill of a new thought. A good teacher is a bit of a ham. He is probably oversold on the importance and originality of his own thought, and he is sometimes pathetic in his search for immortality through his students. With it all, teaching affords him more chance to give of himself, both in his learning and in his loving, than just about any other field. That includes the restaurant field, I remind myself tonight.

Sunday, March 11

This was the first Sunday I had worked required hours since 1945. It's a different feeling from working voluntarily on that day. I passed Bostonians on their way to church as I walked to work. I told myself that I made it possible for them to go to pray by having lunch ready for them when they were done. It's surprisingly easy to prove that one is doing the Lord's work.

The day had its own rhythm, quite different from the rest of the week. It started later. Few customers came in before 1:00; the sermons must be long in Boston. But, once the pace quickened, it never let up until 9:00. There was none of that mid-afternoon lull which I had used on other days to catch up on my supplies. Apparently, there is no such thing as a normal eating hour on Sunday afternoons.

I walked into the kitchen this morning with the extra confidence that comes from three days' knowledge of the job. I felt some pride in being a cook's helper. But the first order of the day set me back. Some kid ordered a peanut butter and jelly sandwich. That's where pride ends for a sandwich man.

Maybe the poor kid didn't know any better. But why do adults come into a seafood restaurant like this and order a hamburger or an egg-salad sandwich on toast? I suppose part of the reason is the long ties here with the past. The guidebooks say that the Oyster House "is not to be missed"; they don't say that you have to like seafood to get in.

One thing I learned quickly in the kitchen is that customers are being graded from the time they come in that front door. What they order and how they order it is what counts most, up until tipping time. Let a customer show ignorance of scrod or ask to substitute beef on the shore dinner, and he gets assigned to a niche just above the one reserved for the poorest tippers.

I learned too that it really doesn't pay for the customer to be rude to the waitress. He may think he is putting her in her place, but there are subtle ways in which he pays for those airs. The most obvious is that his order may be slower in coming, but that's only the beginning. If the waitress is really offended by his manner, she is likely to be talking about him all the way across the kitchen floor. The cook or the salad man picks up the cue. That heightens the chances that the serving will be smaller, the bread staler, or the seafood less choice. And there's a good chance that the waitress, in picking up the order, will munch a bigger bite of the crab or the French fries from the plate than she would were the customer polite. Perhaps good manners don't bring automatic rewards to customers—but bad ones bring swift revenge.

The waitresses here, with two or three exceptions, are over fifty-five or under twenty-five. All are white. The older ones all have long service records. They don't match the oyster shucker downstairs, who had his fiftieth anniversary with the Oyster House last year (that's a lot of oysters!), but they are edging up on him. Without looking busier, they somehow manage to walk circles around the young waitresses in getting their orders into, and their food out of, the kitchen. They don't waste any motion, and they have perfected voices that no cook can avoid. Their incomes show their skill. The best among them make $10,000 or so, I am told.

All their introductions to me were of a pattern and all their names fitted their faces and figures. They didn't give me their names until yesterday or today; maybe they were waiting to see if I stuck it out through those first days. But then the greetings came in a flood.

"I'm Gladys. What's your name?"

"I'm Pearl. What's your name?"
"I'm Ethel. What's your name?"
"I'm Lillian. What's your name?"
"I'm Abbie. What's your name?"
"I'm Moitle. What's your name?"

Myrtle is the house character. She is seventy-five years old, they say, and a former vaudeville star. In spirit she still is, and it is a younger spirit than the rest of us show to the world. Her "Bless you" in thanks for something as routine as a slice of tomato for a hamburger is sincere. And her occasional dance steps as she crosses the kitchen floor are pure joy.

On the other hand, there appear to be three or four of the older waitresses who compete for the title of house bitch. One seems an obvious winner at one moment, only to have her place taken by another a few moments later. They have long enough service records so that they have seen all the cooks except Jacob come as new employees. They have no intention of letting that seniority be forgotten by the cooks, the salad man, or the other waitresses. They are the guardians of tradition for the restaurant, and they are never wrong. If their orders come out mixed up, it is the cook's or the salad man's fault—and that is the way it has been for twenty years.

Their position is a hard one to maintain. They want to be contemptuous toward the kitchen staff (I think that race is more than an incidental factor there), but the job simply won't permit much of that. If they don't make a show of being nice to the cooks, their orders can be slowed down or entirely lost. That makes all the difference between a good day and a bad one for tips. The waitresses know that, so even the crankiest of them tries quick smiles and light banter when her orders are placed. But those attempts are sad ones most times. It is hard to fake respect for others, in the kitchen, in the dining room, or anywhere else.

Yet most of the waitresses here couldn't be pleasanter to work alongside. Ones like Shirley and Ruth, two exceptions to the rule that everyone is either young or old, go out of their way to be kind. They talk in a manner that shows their respect for you and for themselves. They are the ones who sense just the right time to bring Cokes to the kitchen staff when the pressure has built up the most. And they remember the dishwashers as well as the cooks.

The youngest and newest waitress is Karen. She is blond, gentle, and shy. Each order comes from her with a smile. Can she survive here so long as she smiles? And can she make it as a waitress with a voice that, after three days on the job, is still imploring and soft?

Everyone contributed today to a collection for Lonnie, the salad man whose job I now have. He's in a hospital, but no one seems to have a clear picture of what made him collapse on the street. Two of the cooks and the chef have been to see him, and they are guarded about when he'll be back. When the waitresses talk of him they do so with warm regard. They tell me he never gets sore at anyone, even when people mess up his work. Are they telling me something?

One of the house cranks was upset today because I wouldn't cut up the regular tomatoes into wedges for her when the cherry tomatoes for the tossed salads ran out.

"The chef told me I couldn't. He said they're too expensive."

"Well, Lonnie would have done it for us all the same."

Lonnie has a large family and no health-insurance plan. I try to imagine what it must be like to be in that fix. How will he ever pay the hospital bills?

Just how far I am removed from poverty in my life is clear from the fact that I've never been hungry, broke, or seriously in debt. Mary and I scraped when I was in graduate school, but her job as an artist and my veterans' benefits carried us through. When the children were small, our bank balance was perilously close to zero by the end of each month, and there was no longer any reserve tucked away. Yet, once again, we weren't poor.

I wonder sometimes what difference that fact has made in the kind of parent I am. It should have meant, I suppose, that, freed from money woes, I could concentrate more on being a father in all the ways that go beyond supplying bread and clothes. But, as I look back, I'm sure now that I never gave parenthood the time it deserved. There would be times when I threw myself wholeheartedly into being with my children—making up stories for them, writing plays for the whole family to produce in the living room for Christmas, hiking in the woods—but then there would be long periods when I'd be shut up in my work and out of their lives.

How much it meant to be a parent came home to me at last when my second daughter, Patty, at the age of sixteen left her home with her mother and stepfather to come live with me. I was glad she was coming; it would be nice to have someone else in the big old house where I had rattled around. But I was scared too. Raising a teenage daughter alone suddenly seemed an enormous task.

I'm glad now I had the sense to continue trying to be myself. I told Patty when she came that there weren't rules in the house, but there were expectations about how she'd behave. I wanted her to feel that I was close by if there were some way I could help her find her way, but that I wouldn't push myself into her world. My picture now is that this generally worked well. Our friendship grew deeper each month, and I began to feel important as a steadying, believing person in her world. Developing a good relationship with one child spilled over into better times with all the rest. We have never been poor in money terms. I came to feel that we weren't poor in loving terms either.

Monday, March 12

Today was as quiet as yesterday was rushed. Now I have discovered that this job too can have its crushingly dull times.

The kitchen was noisy enough at the start. The chef and the supply man, Mike, were having a fierce word battle when I came in. I didn't know how it started, and I still don't know how it ended. All I know is that, if either man were as incompetent as the other claimed at the height of the fight, the Oyster House would be out of business by now.

Mike seems to have been here almost forever. He alone knows all the recesses of these old buildings. He does maintenance work as well as buys, stores, and counts all the food and liquor that come in. His day begins at 5:00 A.M. when the fish and vegetable markets come to life; it ends in midafternoon unless a dishwashing machine breaks down just as he is ready to quit. He's fifty-fivish, squat, belligerent, and wool-hatted all day and all year long. His is the loudest voice I've heard since I left Gus Reed in Atlanta.

In the heat of the dispute, the chef and Mike used the standard words I had heard the pipeline crew use. But this was a pale imitation. If these men are going to use obscenities, they need to take lessons before they try the big leagues.

There is constant chatter among the cooks. The waitresses' calls of "Ordering a full steamers on the shore" or "Ordering two baked stuffed haddock" serve to punctuate the chatter, but they don't stop it. These men attend to a bewildering array of orders with speed and poise and never lose track of where they are in their private conversation. Their manner with one another is easy and relaxed. They have an endless supply of anecdotes to fill the day. By five in the afternoon, there are still funny things to be told about their encounters the day before with repairmen, bartenders, and traffic police. I can't figure out how they manage to crowd so much living into so few hours off.

A striking feature of their constant talk is that none of it concerns complaints about the job itself. The only exceptions are a few angry words to waitresses over disputed orders and some asides to me about how hellishly hot the kitchen is in the summertime. There is talk of money, of course, but it is more often directed at how much everything they buy costs than at how little they are paid. I haven't heard any talk of employer unfairness or miserliness so far. If those complaints are there, they don't come out while I'm around. What comes across instead is an impression of men who accept their jobs pretty much as they are and who know they do their work well.

The chef told me he had never known a staff of cooks where absenteeism is less of a problem and where relations within the group are so smooth. That must be a blessing to him. The cooks' work area is crowded; they rub shoulders with one another all day. Bad feelings in such close quarters would be explosive. But these men have worked together long enough that the rough edges in their relations have been rubbed off by now.

I wondered as I watched them work whether these were the jobs they would hold if they were white instead of black. They are clearly fast, intelligent men; they have to be to manage the stations as they do. Their work demands an instant setting of priorities and retentive minds. At least three of them have strong, engaging personalities, and all of them are neat. I tried to imagine these same characteristics in whites; the men I compared them with weren't cooks, because I knew only two male cooks before this, but rather men in executive jobs. Suppose these men had come into the labor market fifteen years later. Wouldn't the new opportunities now open for blacks have meant they'd be moving into positions of major trust? If they stay as cooks, the test of how far they'll go may be one that turns upon how much of an artist each man is. Whatever else their strengths, I do not think any one of them is an artist at heart; if that is the case, cooking will be a job rather than a blossoming career.

But how do I know what they want or esteem? I'm trying to imagine how far they can go. I'm playing the old game of projecting my needs onto other people.

Maybe that's a less dangerous game, however, than the other, more common one in which men in demanding jobs assume that those in less responsible posts are happier.

The myth of the happy worker—in earlier literature, read "the happy peasant"—lives long and dies hard. Its theme is that those whose work seems simple to others are themselves more easily, more fully satisfied by what they do. Thus we are told to believe that most people were happier and more creative in the preindustrial era and that those still closest to the soil and those who make things with their hands (cooks, for example) are most content in our own time. Scholars of economic growth don't help support that myth out of the past; they tell us how hard life was for most of those who lived in "golden ages." But our contemporaries who attack all technology and find the root of today's evil in the machine are resolved to keep the myth alive. They tell us that modern man (woman and child too) is the slave of the machine and the time clock; they forget that earlier man (woman and child too) was more often the slave of the shovel and the hoe than he was an artisan of cathedrals or silverware.

The higher one goes in the pecking order of our society, the more one hears the wish to find the simple joys again. That is part of what brought me here, I suppose. And that is what leads frustrated men in top jobs to dream of jumping over all the in-between jobs to land in what they see as a less demanding spot once again. Rabindranath Tagore illustrates this well. In a society where the status lines are rigidly drawn, this aristocratic Indian poet could write in "Lover's Gift":

> I should gladly suffer the pride of culture to die in my house, if only in some happy future I am born a herd-boy in the Brinda forest.

> The herd-boy who grazes his cattle sitting under the banyan tree, and idly weaves gunja flowers into garlands, who loves to splash and plunge in the Jamuna's cool deep stream. . . .

> No, I will never be the leader, brothers, of this new age of new Bengal; I shall not trouble to light the lamp of culture for the benighted. If only I could be born, under the shady asoka groves, in some village of Brinda, where milk is churned by the maidens!

Apart from being puzzled about why he doesn't consider the possibility that he might be the one doing the churning, I wonder too how happy he would be as a herd-boy for more than a few weeks. My guess is that he would find frustrations, joys, pains, and dreams in just about the same mixture there as in his friends whom he left behind to take up that new life. It is arrogant of him, and of me, to assume that we have a monopoly on problems in the higher-status jobs.

So if I am clearing cobwebs and anxieties out of my mind through this work experience, it is not because I have come to live among simpler, happier, or even better folks. It is because I am not fully engaged here, and their work and a small glimpse of their lives let me see my own work and life in a new light. I'm learning more about what we have in common than about what drives us apart. The truth is that we are all somewhat mixed up—and some of us in both worlds are happy about even that fact.

Tuesday, March 13

I can make a neat club sandwich by now. When it leaves the kitchen, the plastic picks still hold all the parts in place. If friends elsewhere tell me that's no big thing, let them try it. But let them try it under fair conditions: The challenger must come fresh from mixing a bucket of chicken salad, must accept a steady flow of calls that "We're out of cucumber slices" and "Creamers too" in his ears while he works, and must know that there are five pounds of shrimp sitting waiting to be shelled and deveined when the sandwich is done.

The chef is beginning to give me my head. "Do you know how to make coleslaw?"

"Well, I sometimes make it at home."

"Go ahead and make it. We just use mayonnaise, vinegar, and sugar. You'll find cabbage in the cooler."

No proportions. No quantities. Just make coleslaw. It was like sending a kid into F. A. O. Schwarz and saying, "Just shop."

I chose a huge dishpan. After all, this was not like preparing food for the two, three, or four who usually sit at my table at home. I figured the pan would hold five gallons or so and that was how much I'd make.

It was hand-mixed in the most literal sense. The public health department might not have approved. But my arms—washed, I'm quite sure—were into the mayonnaise and cabbage up to the elbows. A glorious, reckless feeling. And the end product tasted quite good. I had some for my lunch.

I enjoyed that enough to ask the chef if he would trust me to make cocktail sauce for the fish.

"Sure. Go right ahead."

One of the cooks told me later that a more accurate answer from the chef would have been, "That's part of your job, man." I promised the chef to make the sauce less hot than I do at home. That was a reasonable concession to make in return for the privilege of making a huge plastic bucket of the stuff all at once.

Joey Milano came by to pick up an order "to go."

"Do you really like it here?"

"Yes, it's a good job, and I like the people I work with. Most of them anyway."

That was a true response.

Wednesday, March 14

A day off.

The Oyster House has been in business since 1826. They have done well without me for all those years. I still wonder tonight how they made it without me today.

In some ways I have a different life here. The work is obviously changed: I get rather than give orders. The clothes are different: the boss chooses what I wear on the job. The hours are shorter: I have no duties for the Oyster House beyond the sixty-plus hours on the time clock. The room where I live is only about the size of one of the thirteen rooms in my campus home.

But there are many ways in which life is the same for me.

Once I close the door of my room on a day off here, I'm not far away from the off-duty world in which I normally live. My portable radio brings me the classical music and wordy talk shows of WGBH, so I don't miss WFLN in Philadelphia. I've got enough of my books with me to feel relaxed. No friends drop in, and there's no telephone (what bliss!) or liquor. But what I'm earning lets me buy some beer and both *The Boston Globe* and *The New York Times*.

A day alone is something that many people may dread. Not me. The plain truth is that I rather enjoy my own company. I have been alone often in recent years; the campus allows me more privacy than I would have guessed. And I can't remember any time when I wished there were more people around.

Only in the last year or so have I come to accept what friends have told me often enough; namely, that I'm hard to know. I used to think that I was in fact the person I first appear to be, an open man with whom one could easily get on close terms. Now I'm forced to admit that, once most people begin to get to know me well, I lower a curtain and keep them away. I don't pretend to know why, and I wish it weren't so. I've got lots of room for more and closer friends.

I'm a born eavesdropper. Sitting in a restaurant or on a train, I am frequently tuning in on conversations not meant for me. More and more I find myself listening for the cues that tell me how much of each person is revealed to the one with whom he or she talks. I haven't learned much that way. I don't often hear people entering into deeper levels of understanding with one another than I think I have with most friends. So I'll have to learn some other way.

Maybe, however, I'll never learn. Maybe this privatism is as much a part of me as anything else.

Certainly I feel at peace tonight, and that means I can't be too much worried by an absence of many truly close friends.

Thursday, March 15

A quiet day, with a dreary rain outdoors and not many customers indoors.

There was time for longer talks on the job.

Etienne is a twenty-one-year-old dishwasher with very long hair and a red band to hold it out of his eyes. He is French, living away now from both his father back in France and his mother and Army stepfather in this country.

"But I'm not going to spend my life in kitchens."

He talks of going to art school this fall. But he is not optimistic about a future in art. "I can't draw people or cars or things like that very well. Someday I'll have an apartment of my own and I'll do a psychedelic wall with black-light paint. That's what I'd really like to do."

His eyes light up, too, when he talks about rock groups and about his own interest in guitar. The theme is the same as when he talks about art: "It's hard to make a living that way too."

This is a nice guy who is adrift and who has no firm idea about how to end the drifting. How many Etiennes have the same unlikely dreams tonight?

For the first time, I wanted to drop my disguise and tell him how many men at Haverford are as much at sea as he is. They are living in fine dormitories, getting good food served to them, and attending classes with some of the country's best teachers; he is living in a cheap flat and washing dishes, hauling garbage, and mopping floors. But many of them are also adrift. The big difference is that they are paying about $4,500 a year for drifting along, and he is earning about one and a half times that a year.

Even if I had dropped the disguise, I wonder if I could have done more for Etienne than I can do for the men back home who are trying to find themselves in a new day. Sometimes a college president feels powerful, capable of moving any mountain except the educational policy committee. Other times, he knows how little he can do. Most hours that I spend with lost students are such times. I can believe in them, hope for them, and wait for them. That is never enough.

In colleges, we have too often thought of psychological and career counseling as a luxury, a frill that detracts from the core educational budget. And, for many students, that is the way such services should be seen; those people either know what they want or at least act as if they know. For many other students, less aggressive and less career-oriented, professional counseling can make a large difference in their adjustment to classes, jobs, and parents alike. A college knows how to do that kind of counseling. What it lacks most often is the will to provide it, and the conviction that it matters enough to justify budgeted support.

But where is the counseling for the Etiennes of the world to come from? Who will stop long enough to say that they too are worthy of help in finding their way? I once heard an Indian socialist define socialism for an American academic audience; he said it meant that the president of that university and its garbage collector should both pay the same price for milk. That would be a radical advance in India. In America, our need may be for a way in which Etienne and a Haverford student have the same access to help in thinking about what to do with their lives. That is radical too, but the alternative is for the gap to get wider between those among us who already have so much and those who still have so little.

There was time too today to talk with John Lambert about how he became a chef.

"I had a brother at Harvard. But I started in a religious order, believe it or not. In California. And there I did kitchen work more than anything else. I liked it. But I left the order. It wasn't for me. I went to work for a private family. After five years of that, they paid my way to the Culinary Institute in New Haven. You go there two years and work in a hotel or restaurant part of the time. I was placed in the Statler hotels. When I finished, they took me on as a sous-chef and shipped me to Buffalo. That's like going nowhere fast. I hated the city. Then they shifted me to Hartford. There's a lot of banquet work there. That's a different kind of hell. But it's still hell.

"I learned they had another transfer in mind for me. This time it was to be Houston. I told them to go screw themselves. Those hotels are all the same. They can't keep good cooks. The ones they have are drunk most of the time, and the absenteeism is terrible. No wonder the banquet food is so lousy. I came from the hotel to here. I'd never go back to that kind of work."

I wondered, however, if there was sufficient challenge in this place to hold him for long. He is young enough and ambitious enough to go far in food. This is a prestigious place for him to be. It must also seem small some days.

Friday, March 16

There is a routine to the days by now. Even the frenzied lunch and dinner hours have a sameness about them. Yet, up to this point, the work never seems dull so long as there is enough to do.

There are just enough items for which the salad man is responsible that some one among them must run out in the busiest times. The list surprised me tonight when I wrote it down:

tuna salad
chicken salad
coleslaw
tartar sauce
cocktail sauce
sliced chicken, ham, and turkey
bacon
cut salad greens and lettuce leaves
sliced cucumbers
pickled cucumber slices
cherry tomatoes
ripe olives
hard-boiled eggs

lobster meat
crabmeat
large and small shrimp
Bermuda onions
mayonnaise
French, Russian, creamy Italian,
    and blue cheese dressings
white, whole wheat, and rye breads
hamburger and hot dog rolls
potato chips
sour cream
whipped cream
gingerbread
shortcake
strawberries
chocolate, butterscotch, and vanilla puddings
apple, cherry, lemon, custard, and Boston cream pies
fruit cocktail
grapefruit
butter
lemon wedges
milk and creamers

I make only the first five of those from scratch, but I also cook the shrimp and the hard-boiled eggs, whip the cream, and fry the bacon. It would be best for the house profits if I didn't fry the bacon; since I learned where to do it, I've put about two pounds under the broiler and left them there so long that they had to be scrapped. If the chef keeps a "Need to Improve" list for his staff, I'm still providing him with entries to make opposite my name.

It suddenly hit me today how very noisy the kitchen is. The world I am used to at Haverford is such a quiet one. In my office the only sounds through the day are the IBM typewriter next door, the loud gong of the grandfather clock each hour, the periodic ring of the telephone outside followed by my secretaries' warm hello, and whatever quiet conversation there is within. In the Oyster House kitchen it's a different world entirely. Muzak is constantly playing above my head, with music from my generation or from the Broadway hit shows of one and two decades ago. One of the cooks has his radio going still louder, tuned to sports broadcasts, soul music, or what seems like an hourly replay of the hit of the day, *Killing Me Softly*. In the busy hours, there is a steady shout of orders. and a reshout of lost orders; and there is the constant flow of social banter. Cooler and range doors bang, frying pans drop, and the steamer lets off steam. And over it all there is the clatter of china and glassware being sorted into trays and the whoosh and swoosh of water in the dish machines. I know I am where the action is here.

Saturday, March 17

St. Patrick's Day in Boston, with heavy rains all day long.

My Orangeman ancestors would have wept to see me wearing the shamrock that Joey placed on each of our uniforms today. I knew, however, that there were enough Irishmen among the bartenders, oystermen, and waitresses not to stir up a fuss.

The waitresses with an Irish lilt to their voices every day found that they had more kinsmen today,

white and black, than they suspected. Almost everyone had a bit of that lilt in his speech by the time the
day was done. And there wasn't anything but praise
of Ireland to be heard in the kitchen at all. Myrtle,
the waitress with the vaudeville past, and I even
managed "When Irish Eyes Are Smiling" in a duet.

The rains did nothing to keep the crowds away.
At one point, people waiting for tables upstairs
stretched all the way downstairs, out the front door,
and along the wet street. I wasn't sure whether this
was a compliment to our chef or a sign that the cooks
at the other restaurants in town were out getting
drunk.

I go through the dining rooms once or twice each
day to get new supplies of lobster from the oyster
bar down below. Each time I am surprised at how
many young people are eating there. The prices are
certainly not low, yet the money flows and flows—
and much of it comes from the blue jeans of men and
women in their early twenties. I still haven't fully
grasped how big the market is among the young in
a country that has become so rich.

But there is another thought as I go through the
dining room. I am afraid of being spotted by someone who will blow my cover. A Haverford student
home on spring vacation, an alumnus from the neigh-
borhood, an M.I.T. or Harvard friend from years ago,
someone who learned economics from my television
films—these are all possibilities. Once somebody says
to a waitress, "Isn't that guy in the white uniform
John Coleman?" the game is up. I would have to quit
at once. As Jack Coleman, salad man, I have a chance

of being accepted for myself. As John Coleman, college president playing at being salad man, all bets are off.

Probably, though, my uniform is the best disguise I could have. People in restaurants seldom look at the faces of those who wait on their table. They have still less reason to look at a busboy or a salad man. In their eyes, I become a nonperson when I put on white. There's no more color to me then than there is to my clothes. I'm conscious of that in the way I walk through the dining room and down the stairs. I step aside quickly and modestly for anyone else in my path. In effect, I say to those whom I meet, "There's nobody here." I suppose that, had I lived in an earlier time, I would have pulled my forelock when my master went by.

This role takes some getting used to. At the college I have become accustomed to being noticed when I walk in a room. I sense a slight stir, a turn of a head here or there, even a calm sometimes that I never noticed on entering a room before I took the presidency. I don't think I just imagine this awareness, happy or not, that "Jack Coleman is here." I know that part of my pride stems from having a job for which there is wide respect and which attracts attention to itself. So esteem feeds on esteem, and I become in part what people think I am.

But then I wonder where the role ends and the real person begins. There are countless expectations about how I'll fill my job. I still want to believe that I have stayed true to myself and that most times I have acted out of personal conviction, not out of a desire to please others. That gets easier the older I get.

Sunday, March 18

I would feel cheated if I had lived out my life without experiencing a day like today.

Saturday's crowds or poor inventory policy or a combination of the two left us short of almost everything today except for the seafood itself. On Sunday there is no way to get new stocks. We must wait until the markets open on Monday morning.

In spite of radio warnings of snow, the dining rooms were packed from 1:00 until 9:00. The first sign that we were in trouble came about 2:00. The early warning came from the cherry tomatoes. One of them goes in each of the tossed salads, and one of the tossed salads goes with almost every plate of food. The crisis atmosphere generated by the news that there were no more tomatoes so early in the day was startling. Shock on all sides. But that event was followed hard by the news that the cucumbers had also given out. A slice of them goes in each salad too.

Now it was like moving into blitz conditions in wartime.

"What are we supposed to do?" one of the waitresses moaned. "Tossed salads always have a tomato and a piece of cucumber." I saw almost 150 years of Oyster House history being swept away in one evening.

"We'll just make do without them," another

said. She was the type who sang "There'll Always Be an England" in London's air-raid shelters in 1943.

"But we *can't* serve just plain lettuce," the first one sighed.

Fortunately, that possibility was soon removed. The cut salad greens ran out about 4:00. We had had only four or five plastic bags of them to start the day, and that was nowhere near enough. Rationing the dwindling stock had failed dismally; no waitress was going to give *her* customers less than a full bowl of greens. But we still had a substitute: we could fall back on chopping up the two cases of whole lettuce that lay on the cooler's shelves.

I chopped up the heads and washed them as fast as I could, all the while trying to keep up with the sandwich orders coming in.

"We're out of salad," each new waitress coming on duty called out. That was like calling the civil defense office to alert them that the enemy was coming while the volunteers there were fighting a pitched battle in the headquarters yard itself.

"I know already," I called out from the cutting table in the back.

I cut not only the lettuce but my hand as well. Band-Aids didn't stem the flow of blood as fast as I thought they would. I wondered when the first-aid corps would come by.

The last piece of the newly chopped lettuce went into the dining room about 6:30. We then brought in reinforcements: the assistant manager went out to see what he could forage from other restaurants in the area. They were under attack too, and eight heads were all they could spare. That bought us half an hour of respite. I combed the garbage for some outer leaves that I had rejected earlier as being below the house standard. They were pressed into service now. I think I even washed them first.

Meanwhile, there was news of fresh disasters. The strawberry shortcake gave out for a full two hours, until the chef was able to bake more. One waitress in that period managed to sell a customer a shortcake using cornbread as the base. I hoped someone would cite her later for exceptional service under fire.

The Boston cream pie ran out about 6:00. The whole wheat bread and the rye went at about the same time. The stock of sour-cream cups and whipping cream had disappeared while I was chopping lettuce, and there was a long period before I got around to fixing more.

The dinner noise got louder.

"Two chicken club sandwiches, no mayonnaise on one."

"There's no butterscotch pudding here."

"Could you just slice one tomato for a customer who insists on a salad?"

"Toast for Newburg."

"Give me a deluxe shrimp cocktail. But take your time—the old goat can wait."

"I know you're busy, but can you open this fruit salad jar?"

"A lady says the crab tastes funny."

"Is there any more gingerbread?"

"Half a grapefruit."

"Where's my crabmeat salad? Who's the bitch that picked it up?"

One good thing was that, once we ran out of salad greens, no one but me knew that we were out of French dressing too.

And so it went all evening long. Surprisingly, no one suffered much shock once that first terrible news about the cherry tomatoes had sunk in. It was chins up and into the fray from then on.

I had been wondering what the assistant manager does besides look stern, unlock the lobster safe. and borrow lettuce. I found out in the midst of the panic that he was the one to whom I should report that the seat in the men's toilet had fallen off. (I forget how I had time to discover that casualty.)

It was a cold and clear night when I came out at 9:45. There was a full moon over the plaza. The promised snow hadn't amounted to anything at all. But the square was empty just the same. We had met the enemy, and they had run.

Monday, March 19

After yesterday's rush, this was a strange day to learn that those of us on six-day weeks are being cut back to five-and-a-half day weeks "until the summer when we're busier." So Mondays are half days for me from now on.

There was a very big new dishwasher, Gary, today. His voice is loud and his personality is expansive. He is one of those people who make friends wherever they go almost in spite of themselves. Maybe other dishwashers are resigned to the fact that they are near-outcasts ("We're the scum of the earth and there's always somebody around to remind us of it," I heard one of them say last week) —but not Gary. He's bubbling and bouncing whether anyone values him or not.

He seems to be about twenty-one and weighs perhaps 300 pounds. He has held a number of dishwasher jobs before. He hasn't finished high school but is taking an equivalency program instead.

"I'm taking history now. Everything up to the U.S. We're doing the Middle Ages this week. That's the dullest part. Even the people who lived then must have known it was dull. Except for the popes. I never knew how strong they were. Some of them just about ruled Europe. I liked the stories about them. I liked the parts about the witches too. But the rest isn't all that good. I like to read, though, I've got more books than I ever get around to read. My girlfriend thinks that's crazy."

"What do you read?"

"Mostly Hemingway and Fitzgerald right now. I really liked *For Whom the Bell Tolls.*"

"Have you tried *The Sun Also Rises?*"

"No. but somebody else told me about it too. It must be good. I tried Shakespeare, but I didn't go for it. *Hamlet* was the wrong place to start, I guess. Then I read *Midnight's Summer Dream,* which was okay. But *Romeo and Juliet* was too far out for me. Talk about a couple of weirdos—those two were it for sure. But I still like reading."

Gary and Etienne represent the young type found among the dishwashers. They are clear in their minds that they won't be doing this work for long. They do not know their path out of the kitchen or the time when the next door will open, but they tell themselves that the day will come.

Ollie and David represent the older type. A good part of life has gone by for them now, one because he is at retirement age and the other because he just isn't ready to cope with this world. They may leave this particular kitchen someday when the strain is too great—but another kitchen door will open up right afterward, and another one after that.

I wondered as I watched all of them how long I could do their work. I would gladly have held onto that job at Stuart's Restaurant if I hadn't been fired so fast. But that would have been for only a few weeks. Could I stick it out for long months, or for years, if that were all the work I could get? I *think* the answer is yes, but I wouldn't put money on it tonight.

I suspect that there too, in the beginning at least, I'd be plagued by the same question of excellence that is with me everywhere else.

On one of my first days at Haverford, an alumnus who loved the college very much took me out for a drink and for an expression of his hopes for my term. He talked at some length about why Haverford meant so much to him.

"But what do you expect of me?" I asked at last.
"Excellence."

His word keeps coming back. More than once in a time of decision, I have asked myself what an excellent solution would look like. Occasionally at the end of the day I have even walked home past the grove of trees back of Barclay Hall and asked myself, "Was I excellent today?" The answer is irrelevant; it's the question that matters.

I wonder what excellence is in dishwashing.

Tuesday, March 20

The days pass quickly.

I'm deep enough into this job by now that my mind can wander off to other worlds even while I'm filling a backlog of orders. I don't have a list in front of me any more. This is progress.

It's also the best single measure of how different this work is from my usual kind. More dramatic than the contrast in what I do, what I wear, or where I find my direction is the jump from a world of so much paper to one of none at all. I imagine my secretaries would appreciate this change even more than I. There's not a single thing to be filed at the close of the day.

That's the part of this job my grandfather would have understood best. He was illiterate until the last years of his life when he asked his wife to teach him to read. He was a cook in mining camps before he moved to Copper Cliff. I think he would have coped with the cook's job in the Oyster House faster than I could. He would have had to, for there was no crutch of the written word available for him.

A day off. A chance to sample again how complete a city Boston is. Perhaps, with San Francisco, our only one.

There was time to think more clearly about how I came to be here today at all.

This leave was a long time in taking shape. The idea of doing manual labor came as long ago as 1968, but it was vague in my mind then. From the outset, I loved the Haverford job more than anything else I had done and I desperately wanted to do well at it. The first year and more were a honeymoon period when accolades were common for just about anything I did.

Yet even in the first year in office, well before the honeymoon ended, I felt some subtle changes in myself that I didn't like. In one way my contacts were broader than ever; the title of college president opens up a lot of doors and brings a lot of invitations in the mail. But in other ways the contacts were narrower than I had had—for example, in the urban employment programs at the Ford Foundation, in my extracurricular work in race relations, labor arbitration, and television in Pittsburgh, or in the years I spent on labor-union research in Boston. Neither in my social contacts nor in my limited community activities was I meeting as broad a spectrum of Americans as I once knew. The campus was idyllic. I was settling too comfortably into talking with other people who thought about as I did on most issues. That scared me more as each year went by, because I became increasingly aware of how often we in academics were wrong in our solutions to the problems of the day. We had so much to be humble about each day—especially in economics—but we didn't act that way. We tended to see ourselves as the saviors of mankind rather than as just some more of its servants.

I thought too that I, as president, was getting a particularly inflated picture of who I was and of what I could do. When you hear yourself praised enough, you begin to take the praise seriously. I had no one to play the role that Alben Barkley played in President Truman's first days in the White House. Barkley is supposed to have told the new president that people would now change toward him and tell him that he was just about the greatest person around. "But you and I both know you ain't," Barkley concluded.

The loneliness of the top office is a familiar theme in books on organizations. Reading about it is different from living with it. I was naïve enough to think that I could be both the president of the college and a close friend of the professors. In my mind's eye, I saw my mantle as president set aside when I went to faculty parties. I was wrong. Either I couldn't take the mantle off at all or the faculty still saw it on my shoulders even when I thought I had left it behind. Wherever the fault lay, the result was the same. I was almost always the president and almost never Jack Coleman. There were business messages flowing back and forth even in the most casual talk. I came to accept that in time, but I also knew

I needed some other experiences. I wanted another me to come out from time to time. And that me had to be one far removed from the demands that go with the top of any organization.

This urge to get away, in order to return refreshed, was one that I did not talk aloud about at that time. It was still a pipe dream deep inside me. What I did instead is what teachers and preachers so often do: I recommended it for others. From my inauguration talk onward, I challenged our students to seek a deeper blending of the world outside academics and the world inside.

To the best of my knowledge, I have never made that plea through references to the "real world" outside. Parents, non-college graduates, and commencement speakers do a good job of preserving the belief that the campus is unreal and all the rest of life is real. Whether the theme is one of threat ("Just wait until you get into the real world") or of slush ("Now that you are about to leave us to enter the real world . . ."), the thought is the same. Either way, it is empty. I admit that sometimes, in trying to fight it, I have gone too far in the opposite direction at commencements ("It's just possible that this is the real world you are leaving. Maybe the end purpose of man is to learn."). Yet there is nothing more unreal about a campus than there is about a ditch, a restaurant, or a corporate office. All of them have men and women with dreams and frustrations, fulfillments and pains, certainties and doubts. All of them have people who spend part of each day just putting in time and part of each day living their lives more fully. The college years are years of being as well as of becoming, for faculty, students, and presidents alike, and there is nothing unreal about them.

So the case for a better mix between on-campus and off-campus lives for all of us isn't one that rests on pleas for getting in touch with reality. It is a case that springs instead from an awareness of how much isolation there is in *all* our lives. The numbers of people anywhere who have experiences that cross and recross lines of class, race, or job in anything but the most superficial way are small indeed. It is not that we in academics are more cut off than others. It is rather that there is less excuse for us to live in an isolated way. We teach about the whole world, so it is our business to learn more about it.

Most students who have interrupted the long march from kindergarten to graduate school seem to get more out of college than those who go straight through in lockstep. They have a clearer sense of what they want from college and they bring a more mature range of views into the classroom.

Unfortunately, parents don't like the idea of time out; their very choice of the word "dropout" to describe a daughter or son who leaves formal studies for a while shows their concern. I know this concern at first hand through the words that flowed instinctively from me when my oldest daughter called to say she was taking a leave from Earlham College: "Nancy, I didn't mean *you* when I advocated that students drop out." She proved to be right in taking that leave, and most other students who have done so have been equally right.

Someday we may find a broader recognition of

the need for rhythm in young peoples' lives, the
need for times of deep, disciplined involvement in
formal study and then for times of paid work and
travel of more than a summer's length. The next step
will be to recognize the need for a similar rhythm in
our own lives.

Inside myself, I knew that the advice I was giving to others was really meant for me. I felt I could
do a better job if I got away from the flow of words
and the play of politics for a while. But all of this
remained vague in my mind until the first week of
May in 1970.

Each person has his own climactic event from
the incredible decade between 1960 and 1970, some
event from which he or she dates a critical awareness,
perhaps a new fear or a new hope. For some, that
event may have been the Cuban missile crisis, the
assassination of John Kennedy, Martin Luther King's
"I have a dream" speech, the rioting in Watts, the
first use of napalm in Vietnam, or the slayings in
Attica. For me, it was the news of the attack by
construction workers on peace marchers in the Wall
Street area on May 8, 1970. I read with a sickening
dismay of overalled men banging their hard hats on
the long-haired heads of student activists.

Emotionally, I was with the peace marchers. I
was a fringe part of the peace movement and, like
the students, heartsick by what the Vietnam war
seemed to be doing to us all. But I couldn't iden-
tify that day with one side or the other. Part of me
was on both sides of the clash. There *had* to be a
reason why both groups did what they did. I
couldn't accept the idea that it was a clash between

angels on the one side and devils on the other. The whole thing was as unreal to me as if people in both camps had suddenly started burning their own homes.

I was in New York's Wall Street area about ten days later when the building trades council organized a march on behalf of President Nixon's policies in Vietnam. It wasn't so much a parade of support for anything as it was a demonstration of all-out opposition to the peace movement. I watched that parade with the same sick feeling. There were so many individuals in the march and cheering from the sides whom I thought I would have liked for my neighbors. How had we grown so far apart in this country? High on the girders on some of the unfinished buildings along the way, there were ironworkers banging out a steady beat of support with their tools. So far as I was concerned, that bang of steel on steel was the sound of a nation being torn apart.

There were undoubtedly arrogances on both sides in the clash and in the parade. There must have been deep fears on both sides too. There may also have been some envy flowing back and forth—the students envying the skills and power of the construction workers, the workers envying the economic opportunities of the students. I wished that I understood more of what both sides were saying and feeling.

That was when my resolve to enter the blue-collar world once again, no matter how briefly cr tentatively, changed from a vague thought to a firm commitment to myself. I didn't fancy myself a missionary, a healer, or even a teacher. I still don't. I didn't think I was going to put America together again. My motive was much more selfish than that. I felt compelled to try to learn some lessons forgotten or never understood about the world of work. Until I did that, I'd be less alive than I wanted to be in the rest of the 1970s.

Only once in the two and a half years from that day until I set out on this leave last month did that resolve seem seriously threatened. I know what sabbaticals are supposed to be in the academic world; I should know, because I have asked enough professors what studies they planned to pursue on theirs. So, when a Haverford colleague suggested that I apply to the Danforth Foundation for one of its $5,000 grants for presidents taking leaves, I felt I had to agree. It would have been irresponsible not to do so, I thought, and that was a label that I didn't want pinned on me.

When I get back from this leave, I must write the Danforth people and thank them for passing me by when they gave out their awards. Their money could have ruined it all. The puritanical side of me would have taken over, and I'd have ended up doing something that looked conventionally right on their end-of-leave reports.

As it is, I'm where my heart and head alike tell me I want to be.

Thursday, March 22

The day began quietly. Cold, cutting winds and some light snow kept the customers away at noon.

(We used those same winds and snow to explain why so many customers came in off the streets tonight.)

The Oyster House has a vintage elevator that carries stock and, perhaps illegally, us from floor to floor. There are doors at each landing but they are seldom used. Nor does the elevator have doors of its own. It is simply a wooden platform that goes up and down in response to your pulls (up for down, down for up) on a standing cable that activates the hoist. Just before reaching the floor where you want to stop, you flick a switch beside the cable. Sometimes you stop at the right floor that way.

I had been down on the elevator to get sour cream and coffee creamers from the basement cooler. As I got off, Etienne got on to go down.

A few minutes later there was a yell of pain. On his way back up, he had let one of his feet wander forward a bit. It got caught between the moving platform and the metal lip of the shaft wall on the floor where he was to stop. His boot was ruined. His toes were broken. His foot is in a cast tonight. He'll be off work for a week or more.

Everyone is agreed tonight that he is lucky to have a foot at all. Everyone is also agreed that the elevator is a menace and that something should be done about it. Everyone is agreed finally that nothing will be done; "they" should act, but "they" won't. Someday there will be a serious accident and a state investigation. Things will change at last. Meanwhile, we'll all cluck our tongues, be a bit more careful for a few days, and then go on as usual.

The chef passed the hat to get contributions for

new boots for Etienne. He got about twenty dollars. One waitress asked, "But doesn't he only need one new boot?"

A new dishwasher, sent over by the employment agency, was on the job within an hour. The waters have closed over Etienne and his fate for the time being.

I wondered all week whether anything would be said about the good job everyone had done fighting the battle of the big crowds and the short supplies last Sunday. I knew what I had done and I figured that others must have done still more. Today the first and only reaction came.

The chef called me into the pantry. "We have a meeting every once in a while. The bosses, the hostess, and me. We talk over everybody's gripes. The waitresses were upset about the pantry. The hostess told Joey you haven't kept up the coleslaw and butter supplies in those serving tubs."

"But John, no one told me I was supposed to. And I read that card on the wall that says the bus-boys and waitresses are supposed to do that."

"I know. But it's been changed. They said in particular that last Sunday when they were very busy it was a problem. They were counting on you to keep the tubs filled so that they could get on with their orders."

"Last Sunday? My God!"

"I know."

"Why didn't they come to me about it instead of going all the way around through the hostess?"

"That's not the way they do it."

I was obviously upset.

"Don't take it so hard. They like you. They like your sense of humor."

An expletive from the Atlanta ditches flew from my mouth. I meant it, and it had nothing to do with any sense of humor.

"I know," the chef said, "but don't worry about it."

The same expletive shot out again.

Friday, March 23

Joey brought up the same matter today. By then I was making quick trips into the pantry every once in a while to see that the coleslaw and butter supplies were in good shape. I tried explaining to Joey why I hadn't done so before, and especially not on Sunday. He didn't seem very interested in what the sign said on the wall.

So I told him that the times when the waitresses were busiest might be the same times when I was busiest, and that time spent in the pantry was time taken away from filling their orders back at the sandwich counter. It was all very logical, I felt.

"I know," he said. "Just try and work together."

So that is that.

Looking back now, I'm surprised at how quickly I slipped into the "That's-not-my-job" mold in this incident. Sitting in the president's office, I have regretted that tendency in others, lamenting that people couldn't think in terms of the work to be done rather than in terms of who was supposed to do each little part of the job. But here I was being just as defensive and protective as anyone else. Apparently, it all depends on where you sit how you see these things.

The other surprise in looking back is my expectation that there would be explicit thanks for Sunday's work. It just may be that Joey and John have been conveying appreciation all along, through giving me my head and through staying off my back. Perhaps that is the way things are done here.

Certainly I should be used to silent ways of communicating appreciation by now. My father was a master at it. In all the years I lived at home I heard him express specific pride in what I did only twice. One year I won the district oratorical contest for the area high schools. My school principal told me that I didn't have much chance in the Northern Ontario semifinals to be held in North Bay, ninety miles away. He felt that the girl from Coniston who came second to me in Sudbury was really a better speaker than I was and that, with the extra experience she now had, she would outshine me at the level above. Dad heard all this and broke through a quiet, loving reserve to say, "I think you should go to North Bay." That advice conveyed all the appreciation I needed. I went. I lost to the girl from Coniston and the principal was vindicated. He was also wrong. I won, because Dad told me he believed. That was enough for me, then and now.

That was 1939, I think. The other time when I heard him speak aloud of his faith in his son was a time when I wasn't supposed to hear him at all. In

1952, some months before he suddenly died, I was asked, as a young assistant professor from M.I.T., to talk at a labor–management conference at McGill University in Montreal. Dad and Mother came to meet me there; we were to drive back to Boston together after the talk.

I met them in their hotel room. My talk—I can't remember what it was about—was reported that evening in the *Montreal Star*. There was no mention of this while we were together. But in the normal course of events I went into their bathroom. Through the wall, I heard my father say to my mother that he had seen the story. Again he added just one sentence: "I think he might amount to something." That is encouragement for any man.

There are two small signs that I am being included in the outer edge of the cooks' circle at the Oyster House. Jacob, the senior cook, broiled me a good piece of scrod for lunch. Twice before I had asked if I could have fish, holding out my dish about the way Oliver Twist did. Both times he offered me the employee's menu instead. I turned it down in favor of a sandwich of my own making. But today I thought I'd try asking again. It worked. Giving me the scrod was Jacob's way of taking me into the circle.

Then the chef called the four cooks and me together to point out that there were five dishwashers on duty today, and that we ought to use them in cleaning or other work. There is apparently something wrong about having dishwashers stand idle. When cooks or supervisors stand around, it is considered a resting or creating period; but when dishwashers do so, it is evidence that the work ethic is being undermined.

"Make use of your help. That's what they're there for."

Actually, what they were there for was that somebody had called the USO by mistake and asked if there were a couple of off-duty servicemen who wanted a day's work. It was a case of miscounting who was on hand. I didn't use any of the help, but I felt that I was supposed to.

I tried to imagine how close my association might become with either the cooks or the dishwashers if I stayed here much longer. Sherwood Anderson wrote in *Puzzled America* about his continuing close links with working-class people long after he was a well-established author. "They were and are closer to me, as are men who work in fields, in factories, and shops, than any other class of men or women ever will be." I feel more at home here each day, but I doubt that I could come to say what Anderson said. I know I could have a few close friendships here as I do at home. I can't quite imagine feeling friendship with a class, either here or there.

No one has pushed friendship on me in the kitchen. With the exception of the chef, of one cook, and of a few of the waitresses, everyone has waited until I proved myself before being more than simply polite. I feel now that I am meeting the test, whatever it is. Friendship is coming in quiet ways.

When the conversation here gets away from job-related matters, which is most of the time, the range of views is about the same that I'd expect to hear at home. At the moment, *The Boston Globe* is running a series of articles exploring possible links between the numbers business and the police department in Boston. Kitchen talk uncovers a wide variety of responses from shock and indignation at the police to shock and indignation at the *Globe*. There is a permanent floating pool going on within the staff, based on digits in the state lottery; among its members are some who think the police department needs a good shaking up and some who ask what difference it all makes. So even the gamblers in our midst can't agree.

I have heard talk about schooling, busing, welfare, taxation, Billy Graham, diets, and the Red Sox that has shown a similar range of views. If there is a working-class view on these matters, that word hasn't reached the Oyster House yet.

Saturday, March 24

The day began badly. The traffic was expected to be heavy. There was a Bruins game at the Boston Garden in the afternoon and a Celtics game at night. The Garden is close enough to have an impact on our trade. At 11:30 when I punched in, there were grumpy faces and loud voices on all sides.

The chef and the supply man were battling again. How this rivalry started is unknown to me. Perhaps it stemmed from Mike's much longer service here and the chef's arrival as top man not long ago. Perhaps it grew out of differences in style: the older, gruffer, baggier Mike versus the younger, more artistic, neater chef. Perhaps the problem is built into the jobs: the supply man is responsible for everything being there on time, but the chef finally decides what is needed at all. Or perhaps it is just that they are both hard-working, temperamental guys caught in a very small space. Whatever it is, I can picture the fights going on as long as they both stay. And I picture someone like myself thinking they are both good men.

Sometimes their fights are funny. The insults are witty, and both men have their eyes on the small audience more than on each other. Today was different. Whatever the roots of the quarrel, these were now angry men. The barbs cut deep, and the men looked at one another when they threw them across. The audience was no longer appreciative; it was embarrassed instead.

We all caught the mood, me above all. There are two daytime waitresses who set my teeth on edge. (They have two nighttime counterparts, but I'm more relaxed by then.) They gave me my first orders today. With them, "orders" is the appropriate word. How can some people say "Ordering a turkey sandwich and a hearts of lettuce" in a way that makes it the most reasonable request in the world, and others speak the same line so that it degrades and provokes? The latter is a cultivated art. A few people here have been cultivating it for a long time. When the two on duty today gave me their orders, I did what they told me to do, but I was unhappy about them and the world. It was stupid to work in a place like this with women like that; I'd be better off back at Haverford, I thought.

For several hours there was no light banter or teasing in the kitchen. We put in our time, turned out the orders, and waited for night.

Then it changed. One waitress, Polly, came on about 5:00. She seemed to size up the situation at once, and she turned on the charm. Her warmth and her fun were irresistible. Her round face set off by dark, curly hair had a puckish look as she found ways to kid each of us and herself too. The grumps disappeared.

One person had changed the whole mood. I asked her how she did it.

"I just come to work saying I'm going to enjoy myself. And I stay out of the way of the ones that I know I'll fight with. There are a couple in the day that I couldn't work beside. But there's a way to get along with everyone else. It all works out."

It ended as a day that was frenzied but good. It all worked out.

Sunday, March 25

A morning of exultant beauty—that first deep feel of spring. Those of us raised farther north may have more sensitive antennae about spring. We know what winter's grip means and how strong that grip can be. We're less likely to be fooled by the first hints of a thaw and more ready for the return of deep, biting frost. But we also know when winter's back is broken and the ground will soften at last. We know that a day like today can be followed by a flurry of cold—but we know too that winter is licked once there's just one day like this.

I walked to work. I crossed Boston Common and the whole of outdoors was alive. I wanted to stay and just watch. But I'm compulsive about being on time.

It was a heavy day at the Oyster House. The crowds never let up.

I'm pleased that I can take such a day in stride. I've lost weight since I came on this leave. That may not mean much to me, but it will make Dr. Fisher rejoice when I go for my checkup next time. I wish I were going to take my annual exam right now, because I've never felt more fit. Once you find a good family doctor, it's important to keep him happy —and Dr. Fisher likes his patients lean.

There was just one cook on duty when I came in. That's the usual routine. Jacob, the oldest cook, gets there first. He may come as early as 8:00 to make the day's puddings and prepare some stocks. Ordinarily he leaves around 5:00. But tonight he was still there at 9:30 when I left the floor. He looked no more tired, and no more fresh, than when he first said to me, "How are you, my friend?" when the day began.

How old is this man? Sixty-five? Maybe seventy? He has been here over twenty years, but that is all I know. He never stops work during the day. The rest of us run out of things to do in the afternoon's lull of most days. I find brief times when I have filled enough trays of small cups of tartar sauce, cocktail sauce, and sour cream to fill the refrigerator's shelves, have scrubbed my counter until there is no more dirt to be found, and have plucked the stems from all the cherry tomatoes in the house. Then I just stand and stare. But Jacob never does. If nothing else turns up, he makes fishcakes. Either the market for them is unlimited, or he has the biggest private collection of fishcakes in all of New England.

I wonder if I'll work as steadily at his age.

Monday, March 26

Cold rain after the warmth of Sunday. Spring has pulled back to wait for a while. Few people seemed to want to eat, even Oyster House food. Not many customers, not much excitement, not much work.

This was a half day for me. Because I'd be getting my own dinner on the hot plate back in my room, I slipped over to the Faneuil Hall markets about 2:00 to get a piece of meat and some vegetables. My uniform worked wonders this time. At the three counters where I stopped, I got warm greetings and questions about how business was at the Oyster House. Had I been in my Haverford clothes, I'd have received the polite "May-I-help-you" treatment that I get at the Wayne Farmers' Market near home every Saturday morning at 7:00. But today the butcher and the vegetable men gave me the "Here's-one-of-us" treatment. It felt good.

I didn't pay any less for what I bought. But I

did get told at one counter, "No, you don't want that one," and had a better squash placed in my hand. That's almost the same as paying less.

Tuesday, March 27

One of the waitresses I find hard to take asked me at one point today, "Are you the boy who cuts the lemons?"

"I'm the man who does," I replied.

"Well, there are none cut." There wasn't a hint that she heard my point.

Dana, who has cooked here for twelve years or so, heard that exchange.

"It's no use, Jack," he said when she was gone. "If she doesn't know now, she never will." There was a trace of a smile on his face, but it was a sad look all the same.

In that moment, I learned the full thrust of those billboard ads of a few years ago that said, "BOY. Drop out of school and that's what they'll call you the rest of your life." I had read those ads before with a certain feeling of pride; education matters, they said, and that gave a lift to my field. Today I saw them saying something else. They were untrue in part; it turns out that you'll get called "boy" if you do work that others don't respect even if you have a Ph.D. It isn't education that counts, but the job in which you land. And the ads spoke too of a sad resignation about the world. They assumed that some people just won't learn respect for others, so you should adapt

183

yourself to them. Don't try to change them. Get the right job and they won't call *you* boy any more. They'll save it for the next man.

It isn't just people like this one waitress who learn slowly, if at all. Haverford College has prided itself on being a caring, considerate community in the Quaker tradition for many long years. Yet when I came there I soon learned that the cleaning women in the dormitories were called "wombats" by all the students. No one seemed to know where the name came from or what connection, if any, it had with the dictionary definition. *The American College Dictionary* says a wombat is "any of three species of burrowing marsupials of Australia . . . somewhat resembling ground hogs." The name was just one of Haverford's unexamined ways of doing things.

It didn't take much persuasion to get the name dropped. Today there are few students who remember it at all. But I imagine the cleaning women remember it well.

Certainly I won't forget being called a boy today.

Wednesday, March 28

A day off once again.

I went into a restaurant downtown, the first time since I started work as a sandwich man. My curiosity won out. I ordered a club sandwich just to see how well it held together. It was noon, and I knew the man or woman in the kitchen must be having a rough time at that hour, but I ordered it just the same.

The sandwich looked fine, and its ingredients were fresh. I sent my compliments to the sandwich man, but I think the waitress thought I was nuts.

The place where I really wanted to eat was the Oyster House. I wanted to sit down at one of the tables and have someone—one of the many waitresses I like—bring me the menu. I wanted to order that stuffed fillet of sole, after some oysters at the bar. And I wanted the salad on the side, complete with cherry tomato and cucumber slice, and blue cheese dressing on top. I know some of the inside secrets of the place. I know, for example, that yesterday a customer got a thumbtack in his corn chowder (he was very nice about it). But I know too that the sanitation is generally good and that the people who work here care. I just wanted to see the whole meal come together as a production, fashioned by people whom I knew.

I'll eat there someday as a customer. And nothing that happens will escape my eye.

Thursday, March 29

I picked up last week's paycheck today. Since that was the first full week on the reduced five-and-a-half-day week, it is the fairest test of what I'm earning here at this time of year.

The time clock gave me credit for fifty-one and a half hours; there's no pay for the lunch hour each day. Thirty-six of those hours were at the $2.75 rate; the rest were at time and a half. There was also a mysterious $2.50 credited to me under the heading of "Other earnings"; I wonder how many workers like me don't really understand their paycheck stubs. That gave me gross earnings of $164.41. Federal and state taxes took $41.17 out of that. Another $20.85 went to the employment agency, one of the six such payments that I am to make. The net result was that I got $102.39 as take-home pay.

In my case, that's not bad because my out-of-pocket expenses for these weeks are low. My room is twenty-seven dollars a week; I could have lowered that rent had I signed a longer contract or been willing to share a bath. I'm eating only two meals a day, and the Oyster House supplies one of those on five days of the week. I walk to or from work about half the time. I don't need any new off-duty clothes now, and the boss supplies the on-duty clothes. I have telephone calls home to let my children know I'm alive and well, and I have modest laundry and cleaning bills. I'm not using my car, but there's the storage charge for it at the parking lot. The only other expenses I have are for newspapers, a paperback book or so a week, one movie on Wednesdays, and beer.

It looks about like this:

Room, with utilities	$27.00
Food: breakfast each day, plus two dinners a week	12.50

Beer	1.60
Newspapers, books	3.00
Subway, one way each day	1.50
Movie	2.50
Telephone calls	1.90
Laundry, cleaning	2.00
Storage of car	6.00
	$58.00

So on the surface I'm clearing $44 a week.

Yet the message of those numbers to me is not how well I am doing but how big an adjustment it would be for me to live on $2.75 an hour, even with overtime pay. I've made no allowances for insurance, health care, or upkeep of the car; most important, I'm omitting support and education for my children. Those items are all coming out of my Haverford salary. What I've listed is a one-man budget on a short Boston stay. The happiness I have on it is clearly a product of the knowledge that it will soon end.

I realize that $5,200 a year in take-home pay is little enough. What sobers me still more is that I am one of the better-paid men and women in this type of work in town. The next step down in the Oyster House would take me to $2.40 an hour; the next step down at most other places in Boston would take me close to $2.00. How would I make out on that? Many people do. I suppose I could if I had to—it would just be to keep alive and not really to live. In that sense I'm spoiled by all that I've had before.

I am impressed by the yawning gap between what I earn here and what I earn in my other life.

I don't deny that my job at the college has more responsibility in it. The worst I could do at the Oyster House is to be unsanitary; in that case, I'd be fired at once, and no one would know the difference but me. I could do a lot more damage at Haverford —give a man or woman tenure who didn't deserve it and commit the college to half a million dollars in salaries over the next thirty years; offend a major donor in such a way that he'd never come back into the fold; alienate the faculty on a key educational matter so that they'd refuse to trust me again; or fail to seize a chance to lift the college's sights beyond a too easy acceptance of the status quo. Moreover, it would be hard to fire me by putting two dollars in my hand and saying, "I'm afraid you won't do." The consequences of an outright error or even a failure of nerve on my part are great enough to tell me that my salary should be high.

But why is it as high as it is? After taxes, I take home as president almost six times what the salad man makes, and I have some royalties, director's fees, and interest income as well. Nor is that all. I get fringe benefits at Haverford beyond anything the Oyster House could pay. And I get a flood of little extras that add up to income too: the chef in the dining center at the college knows what kind of sandwiches I like, I get frequent trips on college business to cities that I enjoy, the Federal Reserve Bank drives its chairman home from meetings downtown, and on and on it goes.

Surely it would be hard to argue that I need that much to induce me to give Haverford my best work.

I believe I'd try just as hard for lower pay and, conversely, that I'd refuse a less interesting job for twice the pay. Nor do I think I'm alone. Still, I don't often turn down salary increases along the way.

Friday, March 30

Some days go well right from the start. This was one. We were busy, but there was good spirit in the kitchen all day long. The banter was quick, light, and seldom unkind.

I'm trying not to let my knowledge of economics get in the way of learning the business here. Yet sometimes I do get confused about why things are done as they are.

The owners have some interesting ways of saving on the supply bills. At the moment they are worrying about the large amount of Russian dressing we use each day. So I have orders to thin it out a bit with heavy cream. The cost of the cream doesn't enter into the matter; the dressing bill will be down next week, and that's enough.

A while ago they were after the chef for the heavy onion consumption. Most of those onions, which have been rising sharply in price this spring, go into the clam chowder. So he cut back on the onions and kept up the chowder's quality by substituting more clams. Clams are also climbing rapidly in price. Yet there was happiness downstairs; the onion bill was down.

But I tell myself not to knock it. This place seems to be doing well without my brand of economics. The house hasn't been here all these years for nothing. Better leave well enough alone.

Saturday, March 31

Some days, on the other hand, just go badly from the outset. This was one of those.

It was clear from the start that the chef was in a bad mood, and that his mood would affect us all. He's usually so bouncy and bright, except when he fights with Mike, that it comes as a shock when he's not. He has always been pleasant to me, but he had no time for that today. As I watched the impact of his mood spread, I thought about how contagious my grumpy days must be back at Haverford. The trouble is that when the boss is upset there's no one around to give him a shaking, or to tease him into a better mood.

The chef and Mike fought, of course. I suspect that some issue had arisen between the chef and Joey earlier, and perhaps between two of the owners before that. The universal thump was being passed along. The dishwashers finally caught most of it, and they had no one else to kick around. The chef would be relaxed with them one minute and bawl them out the next. "When I say I want the floor swept. I want it swept. And mopped too. Do you hear me? If you don't like it here, you can go out the same door you came in."

David, one of the dishwashers, took him up on

it. This is a nervous, tormented man. He is about forty, tall, dark, painfully thin, and ghostly pale. He seldom lifts his eyes from his work and has not smiled since I have known him. He seldom speaks, and never on his own initiative. He has sat with two or three of us in our dressing room upstairs at lunchtime, spooned the employees' menu into his mouth, kept his eyes on his plate until the break was done, and gone back downstairs to work without saying a word.

That's the way it was today, but with a difference at the end. We were talking at lunch about the chef's mood. Ollie, the oldest and stablest but not the fastest of the dish crew, had caught most of the fire from the chef. He was sore about it. But he had a philosophical view too.

"Oh, hell, we all have days like the chef is having. Can't help it. You just gotta ride them through."

"Was he serious in that stuff about going out the door?"

"I suppose so. He knows he can fire us whenever he wants. And we know we can quit when we choose."

"Wouldn't that hurt you in getting a job elsewhere?"

"Hell, no. They don't ask dishwashers about earlier jobs. They don't give a shit where you came from or where you go."

At that point, David stood up. We had almost forgotten he was there. He changed into his street clothes and silently went out the door into the street. (He was not heard from again during my time at the Oyster House.)

Ollie was philosophical about that too. "What do you suppose is bothering him? Poor guy."

Ollie was in the Navy for many years but not long enough to get a pension. "I could kick my ass for that." Now he is old enough to draw Social Security if he could just give up work. His wife died a couple of years ago. He has a room in the home of friends, but he can't hang around anyone's house all day, so he goes out to a restaurant for coffee early in the morning and sits there until it is time to go to work at noon. He may arrive at the Oyster House as much as one hour before he is due and sit in the changing room hoping somebody comes by to talk with him. I don't know what he does with his days off. At least five times during any busy night, Ollie can be counted on to say; "I'm busy as a one-armed paperhanger with itchy balls." Each time it comes out as a newly found line.

One thing that kept my spirits up somewhat during this day was the knowledge that I was going to a party after work. Josh, the youngest cook, turned thirty a few days ago and he threw a party tonight. I was pleased to be asked. Perhaps it was a blanket invitation to almost everyone around, but I still felt he asked me if I could come in a way that meant he wanted me to say yes. This man has a bright, engaging style that makes you want him for a friend.

I'm conscious enough of race to wonder how the party would go. I soon learned. The shallowness of the restaurant's racial harmony showed through.

The racial structure on the job still puzzles me. The cooks are black. So is Bruce, the other $2.75 man besides myself. All the others—waitresses, bartenders, busboys, oyster shuckers, cashiers, hostess, supply man, dishwashers, owners, and chef—are white. I don't understand Boston's labor market well enough to know how that came about.

To hear the waitresses talk to the cooks across the serving tables, one would think race relations were fine. The waitresses' dependence on the cooks for fast and accurate service makes surface politeness a must. With many of these women, there is more than politeness there; they respect the cooks. But there are others whose polite chitchat proves to be sham.

It was 11:00 tonight when I rode over to Josh's house with three of the waitresses, the chef (now in good mood), and a busboy. (In this one case, "busboy" is more accurate than "busman.") Two of the women and the busboy sat in the front; none of them had shown bigotry on the job that I could see. They apparently felt that this was the time to let it show. We were all white in the car. So the Dorchester area of Boston through which we drove became "Boogyland," those in the street became "boogies," and a trip into their turf became both risky and fun. The chef, the third waitress, and I did not open our mouths. We may have felt guilty, but we certainly didn't say so. The talk in the front seat of the car mixed both contempt for and fear of blacks.

"Look at that one, would you?"

"That one" had probably been drinking. Had he been a white student in Harvard Square, he wouldn't have been worth commenting on.

It was clear that the big interest was in seeking

where Josh lived. Only some sort of jungle hut would have met the expectations in the front seat. We parked no more than sixty feet from his front door. "I'll walk with you," one of the women said to me. There was no one else in sight on the street.

From then on, the evening was something of a bust. Josh's home proved to be one of quality and taste. He occupies the upper two floors of his house and rents out the ground floor. His own quarters are carpeted wall to wall, and the paneling on the stairs and hall is expertly done. (He did it himself.) The living room was small but its colors made it seem larger. There was a well-stocked bar in the corner, and a table of good food in the room next door. There wasn't anything to knock.

Josh's wife was lovely—tall, sinewy, with facial features both graceful and strong. They were a handsome pair. Their black friends were better dressed than any of us were. At first, they looked at us and we looked at them. We commented on how nice Jacob, the cook, looked in a suit. They commented on how nice it was to meet Josh's chef. The blacks got tired of this first and decided it was time to have fun. So they danced in an effortless way that we all knew we couldn't match. For the most part, the whites stood and watched with wan smiles pasted on. Then we decided it was time to go home. As we went downstairs, I didn't see any of the blacks preparing to leave. I think the party was about to begin.

On the way home, there was little talk in the car. We exchanged guesses as to the best route back. But no one wanted to talk about what we had seen. There was nothing to shake our heads about any more.

"Josh is nice," we agreed.

"So's his wife," we went on.

That was the least we could say. I wonder what part of these attitudes a sensitive man like Josh can feel. My guess is that whites hide much less than they think from blacks. I have heard black students at Haverford—and, from an earlier day, Jews, too —tell of the pain they felt in a place where the word "community" too often has meant, "Be like us and you'll get along fine." Much of that pain lay smothered before. Now it is starting to come out. The message from minorities today is that they expect to be respected for what *they* are and not for how close they come to being what *we* are. There's going to be more pain on both sides before that message is heard.

I know now that simply having whites work or study alongside blacks isn't enough. It is possible to be together and still not talk in ways that communicate.

Sunday, April 1

It was hard, steady work all day long.

The rhythm of each day and even of each week is familiar enough that it should be getting boring by now. It doesn't seem that way yet. There is enough variety in the flow of orders and of people too that I seldom feel I have been through all this before. Cleaning up the aluminum trays, where my supplies are kept, at the end of each day is dull; I'd happily skip that if I could. But even in that there is a small element of suspense: the question each time is how far I can get with closing up for the night before the last waitress comes in with an order that requires getting the supplies out again.

I wonder how many loaves of bread and heads of lettuce I'd go through if I stuck at this job until retirement age.

Monday, April 2

Joey and the chef expressed disappointment last week when I told them I would be leaving Boston after work tomorrow. Neither one had said before in so many words that I had done a good job, but both of them now said that I fit in well. The chef had told Joey that he wanted a place for me on his staff after Lonnie came back. I gathered he meant doing something other than washing plates, pots, and pans.

One waitress with whom I had exchanged some harsh words told me at noon today how sorry she was to see me go. I said that I thought I hadn't been very pleasant to her at times.

"Look, you've got the pressure job here," she replied. "You have to blow up sometimes. Otherwise you'd go nuts. That's the way to keep going, Jack. I've been doing this a long time, don't forget."

Another waitress simply said, "I knew you

wouldn't last. You're too nice." I don't know what to make of that.

Nothing pleased me more than to hear I fitted in. Because I liked the people with whom I worked —and liked what I learned from the chef—I wanted to think I could belong in this trade. I realized how much it has mattered to my life to be wholly a part of where I lived or what I did. True, I enjoy being alone at times. But I also want to feel I belong whenever I break out of my shell.

I learned that lesson about belonging in a different experience four years ago. I had been valedictorian for the first class that graduated from Copper Cliff High School in 1939. There were about fifteen of us in the class. Our older brothers and sisters, if they finished high school at all, did so in Sudbury four miles away. Now the International Nickel Company, for whom all of our fathers worked and from whom all community services flowed in this company town, decided to build a high school for us.

In 1969, on the thirtieth anniversary of that first graduation, I was asked to give the commencement talk. I had not been home for more than ten years, not since my brothers, my sisters, and I buried our mother beside our father in a cheerless, wind-swept cemetery nearby. There were no relatives left in the north. But there were some family friends around, and a few of my 1939 classmates were still in town. Not many. Three died in the war that broke out months after we graduated. A few others left for work somewhere else. Those who remained had solid and respected jobs with the nickel company.

Copper Cliff had changed little since 1939. The population was still about 3,500. The rocky hills all around were as bare as ever, victims of the sulfur fumes that have spewed from the smelter for more than seventy years. To tourists passing by the town on the Trans-Canada Highway, this was the way they imagined hell looking after the fires burned out there, but to us the stark hills had a beauty of their own. We had stared at them out of the high school windows long enough that they were a part of us all.

I knew as soon as I came into town that day four years ago that Thomas Wolfe was wrong. You can't go home again? You can't ever leave home.

I arrived assuming that my classmates would be proud of me and of what I had done since I went off to Toronto to college. After all, I was now listed in *Who's Who* and was president of an American college. Even if they had never heard of the college (like so many Americans, they confused it with Harvard when the syllables were pronounced carelessly), it was still a long way for a Copper Cliff boy to go. I was ready for their praise.

What I got was something more lasting. Their message to me was unmistakably this: "It's too bad you couldn't make it in Copper Cliff. But, since you had to leave, isn't it nice that you did well somewhere else?" They knew, as I did too, that I couldn't have made it in that town. The jobs which college-educated men held there weren't for me; I didn't have the practicality to be an engineer, the patience with detail to be an accountant, the interest in health to be a doctor, or the abiding faith to be a minister. The jobs of the non–college educated were also not for me; I'd have needed to be tougher and more skilled with my hands for that.

No, I wouldn't have fitted in there, no matter how much I might have wished to. I'm glad I found a place where I do fit in elsewhere.

Tuesday, April 3

The last day once again.

Joey's parting words to me were that I had been "more than just satisfactory." He said that, if I ever came back to Boston to work, I should try the Oyster House first. That's worth as much as getting an honorary degree any day.

Tonight I dropped my uniform in the dirty linen basket and punched the clock for the last time. The happy news is that Lonnie will be back from the hospital tomorrow and ready to take up his place once again. I looked at the salad bar as I walked out at 10:00. It had been mine for a while, but it was now Lonnie's once more.

Wednesday, April 4　　*Haverford, Pennsylvania*

I drove back to Haverford today. There is a meeting of the Federal Reserve Bank's directors tomorrow morning. That meeting should end by noon. Then I can take off the director's disguise and put on the workman's again.

The time left is so short that I don't want to spend much of it looking for a job. I had enough of that in those three days of walking Boston's streets. So for the past week I have been buying whatever out-of-town papers I could get at a newsstand off Washington Street and studying want ads again. The area around Washington, D.C., looks most promising this time. Unless our directors' meeting is unusually long, I should be there by midafternoon. So I can start the next job hunt before dark.

Tonight I'm in my own home on the campus. There are lights and noises in the dormitories across the cricket field. A few recent issues of the students' newspaper are lying on the coffee table downstairs. The telephone is at my side. It's tempting to get back into Haverford affairs once again. A lot must be happening here.

Maybe one short visit to a dorm. Maybe just one issue of the *News*. Maybe just a couple of calls to colleagues to see how things are doing while I'm away.

But I don't feel ready to come back. Not yet. I went downstairs and turned out all the lights. The president isn't at home.

Three

Thursday, April 5   *College Park, Maryland*

The bank meeting was a good one, I thought.

This is an exciting time for an economist to be alive, provided he is not afraid to say he has been wrong. Most of what we talked about in our meeting on the subject of the money supply, both at home and abroad, touched on areas where economists lately have been in error or at least confused. In fighting inflation, for example, much that we thought was so turns out not to be so after all.

At present I am the only professional economist on the Philadelphia Federal Reserve Bank's board. But I have fellow economists liberally sprinkled among the top bank officers who meet with us every two weeks. Together we put on a good show of knowing what is happening in production, prices, employment, trade flows, and the like. Yet we know —and we know that the other eight directors from business and banking know—that our record for calling the shots is not too good. If we're a humbler breed than we used to be, it's because we have so much to be humble about. That makes the meetings more interesting. We are dealing with matters where there just aren't many right answers lying around.

I'm still proud of my craft. I have never been an exceptionally good economist (I kid myself that is by choice—I had too many other things I wanted to do), but I love the economist's ways of approaching problems. I was lucky enough to be trained by men who never lost sight of the uses to which our knowledge might be put. There are economists so fascinated with building elegant mathematical models for the models' own sake that they add little to man's ability to cope with his world. At the other end of the spectrum, where I'm more at home, there are economists preoccupied with using their knowhow to throw light on the policy choices in resource use for the nation, the family, or the firm. Most times when I stop to figure out how I approached a problem confronting me in my job or my life, I realized that the analytical tools I used—unconsciously, perhaps—were those I acquired in my craft. I think as an economist does. An economist with a heart. I hope.

In that broad sense, I'm an economist all the time. I'm forever analyzing choices in terms of their costs, financial and otherwise. In the more narrow sense of someone thinking, talking, or writing in strictly economic terms, I'm not often an economist any more. I teach one course each semester at Haverford, so that keeps a foot in the field. But, that aside, only the time I spend at the "Fed" gives me much feeling of being a part of the economist's world.

Today there was some of the same unreality that I felt when I went back into the Fed building more than four weeks ago. When I was addressed as "Mr. Chairman" during our meeting, I almost asked, "Who, me?" It had a distinctly different ring to it than "Ordering. . . ."

I looked at my fellow directors with care. I felt proud to serve with them. Every one is a president or chairman of a corporation or bank. (If someone said "Mr. President" in that board room, eight men plus the bank's chief would return the salute.) They have economic interests that don't always coincide with that of the Federal Reserve Bank or the economy as a whole, but I've seen each of them, time and again, put his view of what is best for the economy ahead of what's best for his firm. I know some of the cynicism that's around today about how financial power is used. I credit myself with some sensitivity there, but in working with these men I have yet to see that power abused. Instead, I have seen men who are not ashamed or afraid to serve the public good.

Today I wanted to talk to them, from my experience in Boston, about unemployment. Inflation is the big economic news of our day, both in the bank and beyond. That's understandable. But joblessness is still with us too, particularly among the young and the black. It's just that those out of jobs are usually also out of our sight. But the directors have heard me on this theme before, and so I was silent about it today.

I also wanted to say something on the subject of hard work. Some months before this at one of our meetings, one director expressed regret that some workers who were laid off in his area after a disaster to their plants—"good Pennsylvania Dutch people too!"—wanted to use up their unemployment benefits before they took up new jobs. Their preference to hunt and to fish for a while was a sign of some moral decay, I inferred. Yet my desire to get away from my own job for three months or so was applauded as an understandable need for change. It all depends on who's getting away whether you call it goofing off or not, I suppose. In any event, I had firsthand evidence which I could have shared today that the work ethic is alive and well in at least one sewer crew in the South and one restaurant in the North. But I didn't share any of it. That too can wait.

When I looked at these men today, I wondered how many of them had the same urge I had had to try something else for a while. The fact that none of them had ever said anything about such an urge proved nothing to me. I had never told them of my dreams. Why should they tell me of theirs?

We finished before noon, and I was on my way. I changed from bank director's clothes to job seeker's clothes in the men's room of the Maryland House on Route I-95. It was almost 3:00 when I got close to Washington, D.C. I swung off I-95, found a restaurant with the morning's *Washington Post* for sale, and started to read. The want ads were many and varied, a welcome change from Boston.

I am determined to be out of doors now that

spring is so fully here this far south. That rules out the many calls for help from factories, cleaning firms, and restaurants.

I called three of the construction firms that were advertising for laborers. One had already filled its vacancies and suggested, "Try next week. Or the one after that." A second pushed me hard about what experience I'd had. Zero time spent on building jobs was less than they wanted, I learned. The third was more blunt: "If you've done this before, we'll take you at once. If you haven't, you better let someone else break you in."

At that point I got cold feet about construction anyway. I had ten days left in this part of my leave, and the thought of falling off a scaffold while carrying mortar had little appeal. So I turned to other ads.

There was car washer, a possibility if other things failed. I called a lawn company next; laying sod in the spring sun sounded like pleasant work. The woman on the telephone said there was no one there to talk to until Monday. "But I'm sure they'll want to talk to you then." Another possibility.

Then my eye caught this ad:

"Trash collector. Helpers for refuse truck, no lic. req. 2.50 per hr. 6-day work week. Start immed. Liberty Refuse Co., 61 Cyclops Ave., College Park, Md."

College Park seemed to be only a few miles away on the map. I decided to drive over and try for the job. If I got it, I could stick it out for at least the two days left in this week and try something else on Monday should it prove too hard to take. It would certainly be a different line of work.

Cyclops Avenue was difficult to find. A police officer (three gold stripes) told me there was no such street. A man at the post office knew better. He gave me detailed instructions, but I got lost just the same. A telephone call to the company brought me the last mile.

The street faces the tracks. It is almost entirely unpaved, and the dust clouds swirl to the skies. Most of the lots are filled with cement companies or auto scrap yards. Spring has come to Maryland but you wouldn't know it on this street.

In the midst of the other yards I found one, no more than sixty feet wide, that was more strewn than the others with assorted junk: old wheel hubs, a dead truck or two, rusted garbage bins, cinder blocks, plastic barrels, and throwaway bottles and cans. At the rear of the yard was a decrepit garage. The mailbox out front told me this was the right place. It said "Liberty Refuse Co.," in crude but clear letters. Some of the garbage trucks in the yard were lettered with "Robert's Refuse, Inc.," but the mailbox was surely closer to the facts. After all, it was a postal employee who got me here at all.

The yard, the trucks, and the garage were certainly not what I had in mind when I read that imposing company name in the ad. But I was now in the yard and I wasn't about to run. I had had the same scared feeling inside that I had felt while looking for jobs before, and I tried just as hard to hide it again.

There were five men standing around in the garage. It was still more littered than the yard; now there was an assortment of welding equipment, oil drums, batteries, tires, hand tools, blue work uniforms, sneakers and rubber boots, and a couch that had seen more elegant days, scattered around the place.

There was nothing in the dress of the men or anything else to tell which one, if any, was the boss. I had been around long enough, however, to look to one of the three whites rather than to the two blacks when I asked if the boss were here.

A man called John said he was in charge. He was tall, dark, about thirty-five, and white. He had a good smile. His clothes were no neater than those of the other men, but he wore calf-high cowboy boots. That should have told me he didn't walk a garbage route that day.

I told him I had come in response to the ad, and he immediately gave me an application to fill out and took me to a corner of the garage. I hadn't noticed there was a desk there at all, but, once John cleared away a tire tube, a battery syringe, and some stale coffee cups, I saw that there was indeed some work space underneath. Moreover, a battered ledger on the desk and a time clock on the wall confirmed that this was the company's office space.

The application was exactly the same one I had filled out several times in Boston. But now the questions seemed even less germane. I made up answers once again to tell about "Foreign languages read . . . Spoken . . . Written . . . College education . . .

Subjects studied. . . ." For a man who has prided himself on telling the truth, I'm getting to be a very fast liar. None of the questions I expected to find were there—nothing about ability to lift weights, walk miles, or drive trucks.

John scarcely glanced at the completed form.

"Do you know what this job is like?"

The only garbage experience I had had was one long-remembered work detail in the Canadian Navy. What I remembered best was not the work itself, but the kidding I took from my friends because I had been caught trying to sneak out of another work detail and got put on this one as penalty. But I had said on the application that I had worked briefly as a garbage man "when I first decided to get out of sales."

"I think I do," I told him.

He looked me straight in the eye. "It's all backyard work. The county doesn't allow us to pick up from the curb. Do you understand that?"

I said I did, but I knew I didn't. I'd find out in time.

"I'd like to try." They were the same words I had used with Gus Reed in that Atlanta telephone call.

"Well, I do need a couple of men. I'll put you to work. Come at six tomorrow. Maybe six-fifteen."

There was nothing more to it except for some casual talk about why I wanted to be in the Washington area.

I have a job for at least the next two days. Or longer if I stick it out. It may be a tough job, but the relief of having it at all rather than going through the job-hunting process all over again makes me more relieved than anxious about the work.

I drove around looking for a place to stay. I didn't see any rooming houses until I got to the College Park area near the University of Maryland. Two calls at houses with signs out front brought the same response: there would be rooms available in a few weeks but there were none empty now. I settled for a motel on Route 1 where the huge neon sign outside was of better quality than anything inside. The rate of twelve dollars a night was more than I wanted to pay, but the place was only a five-minute drive from the truck yard and there was a cold beer dispenser just down the road a bit.

"We like cash," the well-bleached, powdered, and rouged motel keeper said. "In advance."

"Do you have a reduced rate for a week's rental?"

"No, we don't have any call for that. But you can pay for several nights at a time if you wish. In advance."

I found the room had a large dark green puddle outside the bathroom door. I went back to ask her about it. I was interrupting a quiz show on television, but she was pleasant enough, I thought. "I'll fix it at once."

She did. She brought a square of red rug to lay over the wet spot on the green rug. Now I have a large dark red puddle outside my bathroom door.

I bought some food to make breakfast in the room tomorrow morning and settled down to read. But my thoughts wouldn't stay on the history of Florence. I began to imagine tomorrow's work.

I had a big breakfast at 5:15. I had no idea when, if at all, we would eat on the job. (I didn't seriously believe those gags about the pay being "$2.50 an hour and all you can eat.") So I stuffed myself with more cereal, rolls, and milk than I would ordinarily eat.

I was at the yard by 6:00. Only two other men were there, and they were asleep in their car. At 6:15 two more men arrived, black like those before them. One asked me if I wanted a job. I told him I thought I already had one. "Okay. The boss must have hired you. I'm Brian, the foreman." He started up three of the trucks in the yard. The clouds of diesel fumes hung heavy in the morning air and cast further gloom over the yard.

At 6:30, John drove in with Joe, the mechanic, and two younger men. A few others drifted in. The crews for the trucks were almost complete. The men ranged from perhaps twenty to fifty years of age. Three, myself included, were white; all the others were black.

I stood around for fifteen minutes or so while the men sorted themselves out into groups of three and got into their trucks. Four trucks left, each with its own sounds of reluctance about going to work that day. No one spoke to me, and I spoke to no one in return. I smiled nervously instead.

Then one of the two white crew members came over. He was short, blond, muscled, and grinning. He looked to be twenty-two or so.

"Ready to go to work? You'll be on my truck."
I was so much older than he that I half expected
him to call me "Pops."

His workshirt told me his name was Steve. The
only other man left in the yard besides John and
Joe was a tall, young black who moved with speed
and grace. He was to be the third member of the
crew. No one introduced us, but later I overheard
Steve call him Kenny.

"We'll be going as soon as the truck is fixed,"
Steve said.

There was only one truck left by then. It was a
rather sad sight. Perhaps it was no more than four
years old, but many miles of driving and many tons
of trash had taken their toll. The roar of its engine
belied its true speed, which proved to be about
thirty miles an hour downhill with a strong wind
behind. The interior of the cab matched the yard
outside in the variety and depth of junk, but girlie
magazines offered added decor. The truck bore no
name on its sides. Too embarrassed, I guess.

When I first read the ad for this job, I imagined
myself riding around in one of those supermonster
trucks that are becoming common as the nation be-
comes more laden with trash. I could even picture
us honking our horn and waving at young women.
But that was not to be. I just hoped my friends
wouldn't see me in this.

It was 7:20 before we were ready to go. One
wheel needed repairs. I was fascinated watching
Joe change the wheel, not because of any special
art to that act, but because of the unlit and well-
chewed cigar that moved ceaselessly back and forth

across his mouth in steady time with his talk. His hair was crewcut and gray, his face round, lined, and tanned. Most of his talk was aimed at the length of Steve's hair. (It didn't look that long to me.) "I never thought I'd see goddamn hippies riding on one of my trucks!" He meant it half in truth, half in jest.

No one told me where we were going once we pulled out of the yard, but Steve made it clear what he expected of me.

"John says you've done this before. I want to see how you keep up with us. If you can't keep up, I'll get you to move the truck. That'll let Kenny and me move fast. Probably I'll teach you to drive it anyway. That's the way I break all of my men in. It's not hard to move it. Most times I'll have it pointed downhill for you. But we gotta move fast."

We rode ten minutes on Routes 1, I-495, and I-95, and turned off at signs pointing to Dryden. This Washington suburb sits on a hillside with middle-class houses, lawns, and dogs all somewhat alike. The streets wind about to suit the terrain. Most of the houses are the same age. Someone planned that they should look different from one another; as a result, they all look about the same. I decided they belong to middle-government officers, highschool teachers, and insurance men hoping to rise.

We made the first stop. I had thought to bring gloves along with the work clothes in my gear, and I had them with me now. I was the only one who pulled gloves on. Each of us took a very large green or orange plastic barrel out of the back of the truck. Each barrel had a hole near the top to hold it by.

Steve took me into the first yard with him. "This

214

is the way it's done," he said as he dumped the contents from three containers at the back door into his tub. Then in a flash he jumped into the barrel and trampled down what was there. "This way we can get more houses in one trip," he said as he jumped. In another flash he was out of the barrel, the load was on his back, and he was off for the house next door.

That was the training course.

He told me which houses to "pull." With three of us on the crew and only two sides to the street, Steve had some maneuvers to work out as to who pulled where. For the most part, he left Kenny on one side and me on the other, while he crossed back and forth to get the trash a few doors ahead of where we were. He also moved the truck.

I don't know just what I expected to find in the first householder's can on my route, but I know I took the lid off gingerly. It was full of garbage. Right on, I thought.

I couldn't quite bring myself to jump in and out of the barrel the way Steve had done. Instead, I pushed down hard with my gloved hand to make room for the next set of cans. With two houses pulled, the barrel was full. I lifted it up to my shoulder with a grunt (that seemed easier than swinging it around and onto my back) and headed for the truck. All kids—and many grown men—have an urge to throw at least one load of garbage into the waiting jaws of a sanitation truck and to pull the lever that sets the compacting unit to work. I threw my first load in with a feeling of fulfillment.

One thing about being a trashman is that, after

your first load, you pretty well know the job. The only progress from then on comes in learning your route, developing your muscles, and picking up speed. I could never have imagined how heavy some of those barrels could be. Most times I got three households' worth of trash into one load, since that was the best way to save time on the route. But sometimes the resulting weight was more than I could lift even to my waist, let alone shoulder high. I had to drag some of those loads down the driveway or across the lawn to the truck. The noise of the barrel being dragged on the road gave me away, of course. Steve smiled patiently at that, and Kenny pretended not to see. It sobered me too to note that, while they never once dragged a load, they both cursed the weight on their backs a couple of times. I knew then that there's no such thing as getting used to what we had to heave.

This work was a far cry from what I had watched the Haverford Township sanitation men do back home. They work hard and fast, and they probably pull a longer route than we do. But their work consists of lifting the householders' cartons or cans from the curb to the truck. They miss the extra miles of walking through yards, the hoisting of loads to the shoulder or back, and the extra physical contact with the trash as it goes from the cans into the barrel. The driver there stays in the truck; perhaps he is someone who has done his share of years on the dirty end of the truck. Here he pulls trash with his crew. Still, I now feel an affinity with the Haverford Township men that I hadn't quite felt before.

Steve was in charge at all times. He directed us where to go, kept tabs on us, and kept the truck moving ahead so that we never had far to walk once we got our loads from the backyards to the street. This has been his route for well over a year and he knows every house on the route well. (We are the only crew working this part of town. The other trucks from Liberty Refuse go to other towns in this county, and the part of Dryden lying across the county line is serviced by some other firm.) He had scared me with that talk early in the morning about keeping up with him. A look at his muscles and the way he moved told me I was in for a test. But, as the day went by, I saw I didn't have to be afraid of him. I was not as fast as he or Kenny, but he never once got on my back. He set an example instead.

Two mysteries about the job were cleared up for me on this first day. One was where we could have lunch. The answer to that one was that we didn't have any. We worked straight through until the route was done. Then we drove back to the yard, punched the clock, and went home to eat as we chose. I was glad my breakfast was big.

The other mystery was about taking care of bodily functions at work. Dryden is strictly residential. There are no gas stations on our route and no cafés. There are woods at the end of a few streets but they're spaced far apart. There didn't seem to be householders who were about to invite us into their homes. But happily we carried our own facilities with us. Next time I see a trashman jump into the open space where the garbage goes at the back of the truck and seem to stare at the curved metal wall in front of him, I'll know he's not looking for flaws. He's taking a leak.

It was after 3:30 when we pulled back into the yard. I knew I had done a day's work. Nothing I saw in the cans today took away from the joy of a big meal tonight, nor did I leave any scraps on my plate. I wasn't going to make extra work for the trashman tomorrow.

Saturday, April 7

When I punched out last night, John told me today would be a breeze.

"You've got our most beautiful route. The three of you ought to clean it up in three hours or so."

That sounded good. We get eight hours of pay for cleaning up our route regardless of how little time it takes. Moreover, Saturday for those who have worked five days earlier in the week is automatically overtime. So three hours of pulling trash and an hour and a half on the run to the dump at the Belair Sanitary Landfill some thirty miles away would gross me twenty dollars today and thirty dollars next Saturday. I'd be back in my room by noon. Not a bad life at all. I wouldn't have thought in advance to call our garbage route beautiful. But all things are relative.

The day worked out almost as well as John said it would, but not quite.

We were an hour late in leaving. Steve had told me to be ready to go at 6:30. But battery problems, a door-handle problem (never solved), and a problem with the two-speed drive (also never solved) kept us in the yard until 7:30.

And Kenny didn't come to work at all. Everyone shows up on Friday; that is payday. Saturday is much less popular. The deal with a no-show is that if the other two men can clean up the route alone they split the missing man's base pay. So there was going to be one third more work for us, but also ten dollars more apiece.

We hauled trash for a solid four hours without a break of any sort except for about five minutes when we stopped at one street's end to talk. I suppose I may have walked further than this before, perhaps in climbs on Mount Katahdin in Maine and Mount Assiniboine in Canada, or perhaps on route marches in the wartime officers' training corps at the University of Toronto. I have carried as heavy loads as these for short times and briefly carried heavier ones in Atlanta five weeks ago. But the combination of distance and weight today was a record for me.

There was every incentive to work fast. The time was ours. If we moved slowly, we hurt only ourselves. If we moved quickly, we cut our day and still got our pay. The swiftness with which Steve moved was contagious too. I caught glimpses of him moving from yard to yard across the street, and I wanted to keep up with him. I succeeded only because he moved the truck in addition to cleaning his side of the street. I still felt that I was moving fast for me.

My shoulder called out for mercy each time I put another full barrel on it, and my legs occasionally shook as I started out to the street. But all the rest of me said, "Go, trashman, go."

I could not have guessed in advance that there would be exhilaration in this. The only past experience with which I could compare it was the cross-country running I did at Cornwallis in Nova Scotia during basic seaman's training with the Canadian Navy. In one of those races, I came in nineteenth out of a field of over 150 men. There were Cokes for the first twenty who finished. I wish I had saved the bottle; that is the only athletic award of my life. Those Haverfordians most committed to a more vigorous program in competitive athletics have felt in the past that they have not had a strong enough friend in the president's office. I know tonight that that may change this fall. But it will be hard to explain that I finally learned the joy of competitive sports on a garbage run in Maryland.

Dump. Lift. Walk. Dump. Lift. Walk. The hours went by with speed.

Saturday meant that most adults were at home on the route. So were school-age children. I thought this might mean more talk back and forth as I made the rounds today. There were many people outdoors, tending to their spring yard chores. Most of them looked friendly enough. While I wouldn't have time to talk at length, there was time to exchange the greetings that go with civilized ways.

That is where I got my shock.

I said hello in quite a few yards before the message sank in that this wasn't the thing to do. Occasionally, I got a straight man-to-man or woman-to-man reply from someone who looked me in the eye, smiled, and asked either "How are you?" or "Isn't this a nice day?" I felt human then. But most often the response was either nothing at all, a look of surprise that I had spoken and used a familiar tongue, or an overly sweet hello.

Both men and women gave me the silent or staring treatment. A woman in housecoat and curlers putting her last tidbit of slops into the pail was startled as I came around the corner of her house. At the sound of my greeting, she gathered her housecoat tightly about her and moved quickly indoors. I heard the lock click. In a way I was flattered by that, even though I had nothing more than picking up her trash on my mind. Another woman had a strange, large animal, more like a vicuña than anything else, in her yard. I asked her what kind of dog it was. She gaped at me. I thought she was hard of hearing and asked my question louder. There was a touch of a shudder before she turned coldly away. A man playing ball with his two young sons looked over in response to my voice, stared without a change of face, and then calmly threw the next ball to one of the boys. And so it went in almost every yard.

The sweet treatment came from women alone. From the way they replied and asked after my health, I knew that at the day's end when they listed the nice things they had done, there would be a place on the list for "I spoke to the trashman today."

I shouldn't have been so caught by surprise. I had read Robert Coles's *The South Goes North* and had been moved by his interview with the Boston garbage collector who said: "I could see the ten- or twelve-year-old kids do one of three things: they'd snicker, or they'd look at you as though you're a freak or something, or they'd feel sorry for you—on their faces it was written the pity they'd have. Well, I didn't want their pity, and I still don't." But reading those things was different from having them happen to me.

Steve spoke spontaneously about these things on the long ride to the dump.

"The way most people look at you you'd think a trashman was a goddamn monster. Say hello and they stare at you in surprise. They don't know we're human. They think that we can carry any load at all, and that we should carry whatever they put out.

"This one lady put cinder blocks in her goddamn can. I said we couldn't take them. She said, 'Who are you to say what goes? You're nothing but a trashman.' I told her, 'Listen, lady, I got an I.Q. of 137, and I graduated near the top of my high school class. I do this for the money, not because it's all I can do.'

"Later that one became friendly and even gave me beer in the summer. I made her think. But most of them don't think of you as a person. I want to tell them, 'Look, I come as clean as you do,' but it wouldn't help. I don't tell anyone I'm a trashman. I say I'm a truck driver. My family knows, but my in-laws don't. If someone comes right out and asks, 'Do you drive for a trash company?' I say yes. I figure we're doing a service that people need, like a policeman or a fireman. I'm not ashamed of it, but I don't go around boasting about it either.

"When John first asked me to work for him—we

used to work at a motorcycle place together—I said, 'Hell, no, I'd never do that.' But they didn't give me the raise I was entitled to at the other place and John promised me good enough money so that I came. The motorcycle people said then they'd pay the same, but it was too late.

"I lost friends when I took the job. Guys would say, 'Look, come and work with me for my old man.' They just assumed I wanted out. I knew it wouldn't work the way they said, so I stayed here. They were surprised as hell, and gradually they dropped me. They don't have room for a trashman among their friends. Fuck them, then. I'm the same as before, and I make as good money as they do.

"A friend of my wife's yelled at her kids one day when they were running out to meet the trash truck. 'Stay away from those trashmen. They're dirty.' I blew up at her. 'They're as good as we are,' I told her. 'You seem to have a lot of sympathy for them,' she said. 'Yes, I do.' But I never told her why.

"I wish they'd change the name of the company. 'Liberty Refuse' sure doesn't help when you have to list your employer somewhere. I took a paycheck for four hundred and twenty dollars to the bank and the clerk just stared at the name. 'Is that a trash company?' she finally asked. 'Yes, but you can see I make good money at it,' I said. That stopped her.

"When I rented my apartment, I changed the name on the application to 'Liberty Trucking Company.' I doubt that they would have rented to me if they knew I was a trashman."

I noticed that, where other employees had their

first names above the left pockets of their blue work-shirts and the company's name on a patch on the right, Steve had just his own name on his shirt. On the right side was a less faded area where a patch had been before.

Our truck was packed full before noon. We made the run to the dump, were back on the route by 1:00, and had finished for the day by 2:00. That was two hours later than I expected from what John had said last night. But after the long days in Atlanta and Boston it felt like a half day at best. I was off on Saturday afternoon, just like at home.

I thought on Thursday night that I might stick at this job for only two days. I was planning to look for something else in tomorrow's want ads, perhaps one of those landscaping jobs. Tonight I feel different.

In these weeks away, I have worked at two jobs which I liked and from which I learned, in Atlanta and Boston. Now I was on one that a man could scarcely say he liked or learned much from except about people and himself. One trek back to the truck with the trash is about like the next one. But I'm going to stay. The exercise is great. The lifting gets easier with every load, even if the left shoulder stays sore. I become faster and neater as time goes by. I'm outdoors in clean air. And, contrary to what people think, I don't get dirty on the job. (I was far dirtier in Atlanta.)

I'm resolved too to go on saying hello in back-yards. It can't hurt, and it still feels right. Frankly, I'm proud. I'm doing an essential task, "like a police-man or a fireman." I left this country a little cleaner than I found it this morning. Not many people can say that tonight.

Sunday, April 8

I read the want ads out of curiosity. Nothing but the landscaping jobs had strong appeal. I'm better off where I am. So it's back to the truck tomorrow.

I read both *The Washington Post* and *The New York Times* in my room. So long as I was into them, my new life was out of my mind. When I carted them at last to lay by the door, I felt a pang of dismay. If everyone in Dryden consumed the same pounds of print, tomorrow will be a heavy day.

In the afternoon, I considered calling on friends in Washington but soon thought better of that. Then I felt an urge to see my routes again and drove over to Dryden instead.

The day was bright. Many people were out of doors, mowing lawns, digging flower beds, and throwing balls. At some houses, boxes and bags of heavy trash and grass—the waste that we wouldn't take from the backyard—were being piled on the curb for the next day.

There was much chatting back and forth in the yards. Dryden looked like a friendly place. My car was washed and my suit, the same one I wore to the bank, was neat. I drove slowly and smiled out the window at anyone near the curbs. A stranger in town, I still got pleasant smiles in return.

Steve had said on Saturday, "This wouldn't be a bad job if it weren't for the equipment." By that test, today was a bust.

Kenny didn't come to work again. A much older black had come back after a first-of-the-month spree, but Steve rejected him as the third man for our crew. So there were two of us again to pull the route. The other trucks left the yard between 6:30 and 7:00. Ours needed repairs. The two-speed drive didn't work again; without it we could get even less speed on the road.

"No problem," said Joe. "We'll fix it right away."

He tackled the job with a confident air. A piece of cigar (it looked like the same one that was there last week) rode rapidly back and forth across his mouth. A stream of jokes, all of them crude and some of them funny, flowed from the cab where he worked. At 7:30 he called the job done.

We were a block away from the yard when smoke began pouring out of the dashboard.

"Abandon ship!" Steve said.

He didn't know I was a Navy type and would take the order literally. I leaped out the door and into the mud by the road. He couldn't see through the smoke in the cab, but something told him I was gone.

The smoke got worse. The captain stayed with his ship as long as he could. But in time Steve too staggered out.

After a while, the air cleared enough to let him

get aboard again and drive the truck slowly back to the yard. Like every good officer, he thought of his men first. He had me ride outside on the helper's stand at the rear.

Joe had wired up the two-speed without passing it through the fusebox. What would have been a burnt fuse under other conditions had become a burnt cable instead.

"No problem," he said. "We'll fix it right away."

John wasn't so optimistic. He saw we were anxious to get on the road, so he told us to take the one spare truck in the yard. "The blue job" had just been overhauled, he said, but there was nothing in its appearance to prove it. Nevertheless, with the help of an extra battery and a jump cable he got it going. Now all it needed was to have its flat tire fixed.

We started out again. The truck was full of trash, so we headed first for the dump.

"The only trouble with this blue truck is that once it stalls you can't get it started again," Steve announced just in time.

We had gone two miles. It stalled at a traffic light. The time was 8:30 by now, rush hour. We were in the left lane at a busy intersection, trying to make the same left turn that most other vehicles wanted to make. The traffic backed up quickly. I wanted to hide.

A school-bus driver threw us a flare. With that lighted, the traffic began to flow around us. We got road service from a gas station nearby. Again with jump cables, the station mechanic got us under way. At a crawl we headed for Bowie and the Belair Landfill there. The truck heaved and sighed as Steve guided it through the muddy ruts that led across the landfill to where the day's dumping was to take place. Obviously, the truck didn't want to be there.

A dump is not a pretty place. To a novice there is a fascinating rhythm about it as the steady streams of trucks flow in and out and the two heavy tractors dart back and forth leveling out the new loads of trash. But to find beauty it is necessary to look up at the blue sky above and the flocks of seagulls gliding back and forth in effortless flight over their food.

At this time of year, a garbageman's job doesn't smell nearly as much as I had expected. A few back-yard cans made me turn up my nose, but most smells were more varied than strong. The dump is different. The noxious odors hang heavy in the air, rich and full. Nor is it possible to turn one's head away, as I could with the more objectionable cans. There was nowhere to find lighter air once we got into those vast acres of waste. The only escape was in dropping the load and getting out of there fast.

That relief is impossible for the attendant who patrols the dump and shows each of the many trucks where to deposit its load. His red plastic cape both identifies him as the traffic man and keeps the sea-gull droppings off his clothes. If I saw this forty-five-year-old white man on the street, with his clean-cut face and well-greased hair, I would never connect him with this job. I wonder how he got there and what pride he is allowed from his work. Someone has tried to elevate the task by giving it a fancy name: he is called a landfill inspector. That's about like calling those of us on the truck environmental control agents.

The dump is so new a world to me that today I just stood gaping while our load dropped to the ground. The volume and variety of what is thrown away are enough to leave me both frightened and sad. My picture of affluence in America is no longer going to be one of all those young people eating in the Oyster House or even of those elegant homes on the Main Line where I live. It will be a livelier, uglier scene: an unending line of refuse trucks spilling their loads of half-used goods on the ground and rushing back to get more before dark.

I lived and worked in India as a consultant for one year. In Calcutta I saw men, women, and children comb through wretched piles of garbage in the streets to extract anything that could possibly be used again. On any one day on this one single dump in America, there are riches enough to lift a thousand Indians' lives toward the stars.

Today I brought back a single souvenir from the mountains of refuse on the dump. I spotted a pile of bold blue-and-white cards with words so fitting for the job I am doing—and the one I'll go back to soon—that I had to take one along. It says: "IF WE DID SOMETHING WRONG, TELL US. IF WE DID SOMETHING RIGHT, TELL US."

I wonder who tells the landfill inspector when he does something right.

It was 10:30 before we got to Dryden and were ready to start on our route. The town has twice-a-week pickup of trash. That means we do a third of the streets each day. I had covered two thirds of the town last Friday and Saturday. This was the last day I'd be going into new terrain.

Once we were onto the route, the fact that the blue truck had no horn, poor brakes, and little drive didn't matter so much. As long as Steve kept the engine going, we could gather our trash.

We worked the route until 2:30. By that time, we had made only a small dent in the day's work, both because the cans were so full (those Sunday papers *are* a chore) and because the truck was so slow. Steve despaired of our finishing at all with this truck and called back to see if the other one were fixed. It was, and we went back to the yard to pick it up. On Friday, it had seemed a wreck to me. After a few hours on the blue truck, the white one was a joy to behold.

Maybe I liked it because Steve taught me to drive it today. Forward only and downhill, but that gave me a sense of tremendous power. At first I felt only fright. I saw this white monster crushing a parked Datsun or even going into the living room of one of the all-too-similar houses at the bottom of the bend on each hill. But I stuck with it because I knew I must. The next thing I knew, I was enjoying the thrill. My youngest son would have smiled with pride —envy, too—if he had seen me then.

We stayed on the route until 4:00. By then it was clear that there was no way to finish the day's streets before dark. There would be no overtime as a result of the breakdowns, so we headed back to the yard. We passed the house of a man in town appointed to monitor our company's work. If he complained because we didn't get to his trash that day, there would be a fine for Liberty Refuse to pay. I suggested to Steve that we make a stop just to empty his cans. He was shocked that I could be so dumb. "Too obvious," he said. On the ride back, I held a wire firmly in my hand. That was how we kept Steve's door closed and him in the cab.

We had a regular day's pay plus ten dollars to show for our work. Actually, there was one dollar more than that. A carpenter working on a new home had some scrap wood to get rid of. We agreed to take it and got a two-dollar tip in return. My half of it was the first such tip of my life. The bill is in my wallet now; it will go to my first grandchild with pride.

That wasn't the only kindness of the day. A man put two beers at the curbside this morning and said how sorry he was that this was all he had on hand. We were lucky there were just two of us on the truck.

That kindness came at a welcome time. Minutes before, I had had a dressing down from one sedate woman with neatly set white hair. My filled barrel had scraped against her expensive and polished car as I struggled to get from her back door through the narrow passageway between her car and the carport wall.

"You've really got to be more careful than that. We just polished the car last week."

I had an urge to swear at both her and her car. But I'm rapidly learning my place. I said I was sorry and it wouldn't happen again.

This day may have been a rough one. But it ended on a high note for me. I asked Steve how I compared with other new crew members three days into the job. Was I up to the average?

"Better," he said with a grin. "That's why I fought to keep you. John wanted to take you for another crew."

Tuesday, April 10

This was a bad-luck day from beginning to end.

My boss, John, is the third one I've had a chance to watch for any length of time since I began this leave. He strikes me as a decent guy who wants to keep his employees reasonably content. He is heavily dependent on them; the job doesn't attract enough applicants for him to be rough on those who come, even if he wanted to. But maybe that stark market truth keeps him from being the manager that he could be if he chose. Four days into the job, I'm looking for the toughness, consistency, and organizing skill that belong with his basic decency if he is going to be a strong leader of men. Still, I like John. I'd work for him again if I had a leave and if he gave me the chance.

John's in a spot. The part of the equipment I see is in bad shape, perhaps because trucks take a merciless beating in work like this. John knows this, and he and the other owners have at least one new truck on order. But he tells us August is the earliest delivery they can get. That is a long time away, with most of the summer's heat and heavier trash yet to come. How many men will he lose in the time in between if the present trucks continue to break down?

One of the better trucks from the other routes was out of service today. That route is much farther away from the yard than ours. So John decided that Clarence, the driver for that crew, should have the better of the two not very good trucks left. He gave him the white one we used to have. That left us the old blue crawler again.

The color was just right. Steve's clothes were blue, and soon the air was too. "How in Christ am I supposed to finish yesterday's route and do today's too with that old fucker?" he moaned. Clarence's smug smile on his way out in the white truck didn't help things one bit.

Then Kenny, who had come back to work and whom Steve wanted again as our third man, was put on another crew. That left us with only the same older man Steve had turned down yesterday. Most of this man's first-of-the-month spree had worn off by now. His eyes weren't fully open, but that didn't keep him from getting around the yard. The only name I heard him called was "Pop." Now I know why Steve didn't call me that when I first came to work; the name was already in use.

By this point the friendship between John and Steve was strained. "If it weren't for the money and my debts, I'd be out of here today. I swear, once our baby's born I'm getting the shit out."

One thing about Steve, though, is that no matter how angry he gets he cools down fast. I could afford to learn that from him. Once he cools down, he has a sense of balance that is rare. He has strong ideas on how a company like this should be run. I can't help but think he'd make a good foreman if someone gave him his head. Certainly he'd have his men working hard.

When we pulled out of the yard (it was 7:30 before the blue truck agreed to go), we had half a load in back from yesterday. That, plus the extra long route we covered today, meant there had to be two trips to the dump in one day. The highest speed that the truck hit on the open road was thirty-five miles an hour, if our gauge could be believed. We saw many other garbage trucks roar past us, proud names emblazoned on their sides. Members of their crews looked out from the cabs and their faces seemed to say, "Man, I wouldn't want your job!" In all, we were more than four hours on the rides to and from the dump. For John's company those hours meant that at least twenty dollars went to two men, Pop and me, who did nothing more than keep Steve company on the runs.

We pulled trash for a total of seven hours. By any reasonable test, that is a full day's work. To-night my muscles confirm that fact. When we finally parked the truck for the night at 6:30, I had had all of this experience that I wanted to have. Yet, some three hours later, I feel set to go at it again. I am ready for tomorrow.

A long day gave me a better chance to make a thorough review of the contents of the cans. We trashmen probably come to know as much about each Dryden family as anyone else, the police included. I'm going to tell the college admissions officers that, if we ever get an applicant from here, I can tell them more about his family's private life than we have any right to know.

Some broad types emerge from all the variety of life-styles revealed in the cans. A few of the more common ones stand out tonight.

The Tidy Tims. Their trash is almost all in paper or plastic bags within the cans. If the bags are paper, they are never wet. If plastic, they are either tied tightly or neatly folded over the tops of the cans. The cans when emptied are clean and dry. There is not a wood scrap, orange peel, or old tricycle wheel lying anywhere in sight. The insides of their houses may or may not be happy, but it's a safe bet that they are tidy spots.

We never get to see what it is that these folks throw away. But if we were to dump one of their bags on the ground, I'd expect to find grapefruit rinds with the fruit eaten away right down to the skin, rinsed-out mayonnaise jars, fully exhausted and carefully coiled toothpaste tubes, and last month's *Good Housekeeping* magazine.

In Dryden, the Tidy Tims' leader is easy to spot. This house hasn't a regular garbage can to be seen. About six feet off the ground on the back wall of the house is a tall metal bin. A long rope hangs from the top of the bin toward the ground. The trashman puts his barrel beneath, pulls the rope with ease, and watches while the trash from the kitchen slides to its rest in the drum. Each day's trash is in dry paper bags, sealed with masking tape on all sides. I wish I were staying here until Christmas; the wrappings on the trash must be glorious then.

The Dirty Dans. There seem to be more of these,

or perhaps they are just a more memorable lot. Their cans are hard to spot amid all the carport and backyard litter. There's a casual air about everything in sight. It is never quite clear what we are to leave or to take. The cans' contents are invariably loose and alternately wet and dry. An old telephone book, some fish and cantaloupe stew, beer cans, shoeboxes and old shoes, dog dung, clippings from the woodshop, sanitary napkins, crayon drawings, TV dinner trays (the peas uneaten), and crushed newspapers have just one thing in common: they are liberally sprinkled with cigarette ashes and butts. The wind blows the papers and unpaid bills about as the trashman dumps the cans into his drum, but he can't tell what part of the mess left behind was there before he came.

I haven't found a clear leader among the town's Dirty Dans. The race is much too close to call that one for sure. But one thing I learned: where there's one Dirty Dan at least one of his immediate neighbors will be the same. This type just can't thrive on a street alone.

The Wet Willies. These are cousins of the Dirty Dans. They leave the lids off their cans so that the spring rains saturate their waste. The cans have a gray uniformity throughout the top halves and pools of sloshing slops below. There is no neat way to deal with their trash. Certainly we can't cart the rainwater away. When I find a can that is heavy with rain, I pour as much of the water as possible on the ground before dumping the rest in my barrel. Necessarily, carrot scrapings and Kleenex flow out onto the ground. The householders who come home at night to find that mess can't help but say, "Why can't that fellow be neater?" If they ever think of me as a person, they probably wonder too what kind of place I live in. I'd feel that same way if I were in the householders' shoes. But this week I'm not; I'm a trash collector instead. So, as I struggle with a load of sopping wet newspapers, I ask myself, "Why can't these people be neater?" But I don't have to wonder what kinds of homes *they* come from. I can see.

The Roguish Robs. These are jolly types who are never at a loss as to what game to play next. Their first game with the trashman is "Guess Where the Trash Cans Are." But that one palls in time, since any garbageman of a few days' experience can sniff out even the most unlikely hiding place.

Of more lasting fun is "What Can We Get Away With?" The object is to get something hauled away that isn't included in the town's contract with our boss. Putting grass or construction dirt in the bottom of the pail and covering it over with paper bags is one way to play, but a garbageman only has to kick the pail lightly to expose that trick. It won't budge when he kicks it. Big points are won only when some extra heavy object is successfully concealed in the middle of the can; the trashman's sure touch with his foot tells him there's something wrong there but he can't figure it out. By the time he does, the contents may be into his barrel, in which case the householder has won. Bricks mixed in with coffee grounds, corncobs, and salad greens are big scorers. So are yard dirt and stones hidden in shoe and dress boxes. I gave the highest points today to the house with a small cast-iron engine block wrapped in a faded old candlewick spread. (My fellow trashmen may object to my publicizing that trick, but then how many houses across the land have those two objects ready to go out on the same day?)

A third game is "Just One Bit More." The trick here is all in the timing. The object is to let the trashman get his heaviest load on his shoulder or back and be just about to disappear out of the yard before calling out, "Oo-hoo, there. Could you take just one bit more?" The smaller that last bit of waste, the higher the score, of course. The game has one heavy cost attached. It requires speaking to the trashman or at least to his back. Worse, he is almost always going to say "Thank you" once his load is set down and the extra bit is dropped in; we're conditioned in our lives to say thank you when we get anything given to us at all. And that in turn means that the housewife, while watching the man struggle to get his load off the ground and onto his shoulder or back again, has to say, "You're welcome." She can't help but feel like a damn fool afterward when she thinks about her words.

Still, life in the homes of the Roguish Robs must be a barrel of fun.

Wednesday, April 11

We managed to get off to a rather early start. We left the yard at 7:20, a record so far. I won't know until I get my paycheck on Friday whether or not I get paid for that hour or so that I stand around at the start of each day.

There was still part of yesterday's route to do. That took the three of us—Pop was with us again—until 10:30 or so. Then we made the run to the dump. We still had the blue truck, so it was a two-hour trip there and back.

By 12:30 we were in Dryden again and ready to begin on today's route. We threw only three barrels apiece into the truck before fresh disaster struck. Part of the drive for the compacting unit had fallen off from under the truck, and there was no way we could put more garbage into the waiting jaws.

We looked everywhere for the missing piece, but without success. Steve found a householder with enough self-confidence to let a trashman in his home. (The man was a retired police chief.) Steve wiped his feet carefully at the door, even though the day was dry, and telephoned back to the yard. It was a full hour before John was located and came to our rescue. He couldn't understand how three grown men could lose the missing joint in the shaft. We couldn't either. But we also couldn't think of anything we had to gain from hiding the damn thing.

John took off in his station wagon to get a replacement part at the supply store. Another hour passed before he returned. He slid under the truck to put the part in place. And then the swearing began. It seemed that the clerk had given him the wrong size piece.

We went back to the yard in John's car and waited for a relief truck to come from Liberty's Rockville headquarters yard. It was a beautiful, gleaming thing. Bold lettering down its side proclaimed, "HELP LIBERTY KEEP AMERICA LITTER-FREE." I walked taller at once, proud that my employer owned such a vehicle.

With the truck, we also acquired two additional crew members. That gave us five men to clean up the unfinished streets. The pace was swift. Steve almost met his match in an equally vigorous young black from the Rockville crew. That race, run on Steve's home field, brought out the best in the rest of us too. We licked everything but the night. At 6:15, the new truck would hold no more and it left with its crew.

John and Joe, wet cigar in place, appeared with the blue truck, now said to be fixed. They wished us good night and left. We pulled trash for another hour in the gathering darkness. Not that we were finished by then. It was that we had no taillights and not much by way of headlights either. It seemed best to get off the road.

As we drove past the Giant market, the parking lot was full. Our customers were there buying more trash for us. They had no way of knowing that we hadn't digested their last donations yet.

Thursday, April 12

Steve and I were alone again today. The attendance record was bad this morning. Perhaps others knew more about the weather ahead than we did.

240

The day began in sunshine, cold but very clear. We were on the road by 7:10, a still better record for us. I sensed my strength growing on the job; there was scarcely a load that I couldn't toss to my shoulder now. I jumped deftly over back fences today, to cut the time from yard to yard, in a way that would have amazed me just one week ago and which the undergraduates at Haverford never will believe of me.

By 11:00, it was raining and snowing at once. It stayed that way most of the rest of the day. It took only one half hour in the wet slush to soak us to the skin. The denim pants and jacket I wore gave in to the rain first. Then I felt the cold water penetrating my shirt and underwear. My feet soon squished in my boots and my hands squished in my gloves.

Along about then, I decided a college presidency wasn't such a bad job after all. I'm seldom out in the rain back home. And six years after I came to Haverford, the college is getting around to fixing the worst of the leaks in the roof of the president's home. The only comfort I found today was in learning that once I was soaking wet the new slush from the sky couldn't do any more harm.

Steve said at one point that the thing to make this day complete would be for the boss to send over rain gear now that we were almost done. He knows this company too well; he had barely spoken when Joe drove up in John's station wagon. He handed us new yellow rain suits. The wet snow made the cigar butt in his mouth a still soggier sight. But Joe was too pleased and proud to care. The beam on his face as we pulled on the waterproof overalls and coats told us that he saw this act of mercy and foresight on his part in the same light as if he had been Florence Nightingale. Inside our suits, the water reached body temperature at last. Outside the wet slush stopped almost at once. The heavens knew when they were licked.

Half an hour later we were done for the day.

I've been interested in watching for the defenses which trashmen build against those who look down on them. I have met men this week who simply close up into themselves once they are on the route, get the job done, and get out of those neighborhoods as fast as they can. I doubt that they even return a greeting in the few cases where the householder extends that courtesy first.

I have heard men in the garage talk among themselves about what's wrong with people who need someone else to kick around. A black man put it best: "Those motherfuckers think I'm coming after their jobs and that I'm going to make them take mine. They're sick." So it is that the scorn gets turned around.

I have listened too to those among us who go that extra mile in asserting pride in themselves. One man spoke of how insulted he was by the woman who said, perhaps with only kindly intent, "Those dresses in the can aren't really very old. Wouldn't you like to take them to your wife?" "Hell," he told us, "my wife won't touch even a new dress unless it costs at least fifteen bucks."

I saw pride asserted in a different way today.

Steve had never spoken to me explicitly about how I was to leave the area around the cans where I dumped. But he made his point more effectively than any lecture could do. He showed me a photo that a housewife had given him of the mess left by one of his helpers earlier last week; his anger that one of his men would do the job that badly was plain to see. He has been on this route eighteen months, and, whatever those on the route think of him, he knows how the job should be done. I know that I took extra pains after seeing that picture. I didn't pick up what the family had strewn about before I came; I don't think Steve did either. But I chased most of what the wind blew away from me as I worked.

I have no idea how many Steves there are on garbage routes today. The one I know may not stay there much longer. He talks either of studying accounting some day or of driving an over-the-road trailer truck. "I know a guy with a really good deal. He makes two overnight runs to South Carolina and makes a pile doing that. And he's home every night of the week but two." Maybe neither of those dreams will come true. But he is likely to do something where he gets as much credit as he gives.

John Gardner has said that a society which lauds its philosophers, whether good or bad, and scorns its plumbers is in for trouble. "Neither its pipes nor its theories will hold water," he warns. He might have gone a step further and called for respect for both our economists and our refuse men; otherwise they'll both leave trash behind.

It was unusually cold when I went to work. There was thick frost on the car windows. But the sky was clear and the air fresh and clean.

Steve and I were alone again. We worked extra hard and fast. It looked as if we would have our first short day of the week. Even the blue truck performed fairly well. Its drive had been fixed enough to let us get higher speeds on the road. We had less than two hours of work left on the route when we set out for the dump. With a ten-dollar bonus for each of us, a trashman's life didn't look half bad. We were a few miles down the road to the dump when, with a clatter and bang, a piston blew. We were doomed. I remembered what the date was. It all fitted.

Steve's anger spilled out all over the road. He came as close to crying as most men ever do. This was all he could take. As soon as he cooled down, he threaded his way on foot across the speeding lanes, went through a small woods to where the state police barracks were, and called for help. In an hour, Joe came to rescue us. He looked at the truck, pronounced it hopeless, and drove us back to the yard with our refuse barrels stowed in the back of his car.

The white truck was fixed enough for us to be able to take it out. Of course, it was full. That meant starting out for the dump all over again. It was about 2:45 when we were back on the route. There were a few long streets and about four courts left to pull.

Still, with any luck at all the two of us could have it all done by 4:30 or so. That wasn't as bad as we had feared for a while when we were waiting on the road for help. Then, just before 3:30, Joe drove over from the garage with an extra man to help us finish up. That would save us twenty minutes or so on the day. I thought, "How nice!" But then I learned that his being there meant that he would count as the third man for the entire day. Our ten-dollar bonus was gone.

I was furious. So was Steve. But he was so surprised at my wrath that he calmed down almost at once and stood back to watch. The whole thing seemed so completely unjust. No one would even know that we had worked extra hard all the rest of the day just to bring us to the point where we now were. At no time in these two months did I feel so helpless and mad. And there was no way I could think of to get my gripe aired.

The sky was still blue and the air still clear, but my head was seething inside. I told Steve I was quitting in any event. (I didn't tell him why.)

He urged me not to. "You're the first good helper I've had in a hell of a long time. Stick it out for a while."

"But you said you were ready to quit too."

"I know. But we can work this out. I can use our gripes about the trucks and that pay to talk to John. With my seniority I'm entitled to a better truck. Let's work on it together."

I told him I was pretty sure to leave after tomorrow anyway.

It was payday. I got $125.14 in take-home pay

for fifty-five hours in six days of work. I was pleased at that. But I still felt cheated out of ten bucks.

It wasn't until I had soaked in the shower back at the motel that I began to get hold of myself. Then the incident came into focus for me. Here I was getting a good salary back at Haverford. I'm a man who hasn't thought much about money anyway and one to whom ten dollars frankly doesn't mean all that much. I had only one more day to work on this job. Why had I become so intensely upset? That is when I saw how involved I had become in this life and this job. It was like those days of looking for work in Boston; I was no longer acting a part. This time I was an aggrieved employee. If ever someone says to me after I go home that I couldn't enter fully into the life of a manual worker in just two months away from my usual comfortable world, I will have to agree in part. But I will also know that there was at least one time when I entered that life fully and passionately.

I learned in that time too. A grievance process came to make still more sense than it had before. I had written of the need for such a system as early as 1951 and in much of what I had written since. I had welcomed the formation of an association of the nonfaculty personnel at Haverford—not because I liked adversary proceedings but because I believed any man or woman in a subordinate position needed a safe and impersonal way to get complaints heard.

Tonight I'm still more in favor of a way to get on-the-job problems out into the open. Many of the staff concerns may not seem big to the man on the top—is ten dollars big or small to someone whose livelihood rests on $2.50 an hour?—but each is real enough to the man or woman with whom it began. What finally emerges as a worker's attitude to a job may have no more important root than his or her feelings toward how a personal, individual concern was heard.

That point in turn has a bearing on how I as a president leave my stamp on a college that I love.

There was a time when I thought that, if I had an impact on Haverford at all, it would be through the big moves I made. A still better teaching faculty, coeducation, diversity in the student body, off-campus involvement, a balanced budget—those would be my key tests. Now I'm no longer so sure. My real stamp may be through much smaller acts. What will last for those who knew me in these years may just be an individual contact, a moment of trust and concern. Ask me now at what single moment I was best in my job, and I think of a time when I learned a particular student was in trouble and alone, caught up in a conflict situation with his parents that tore at his whole life up to that point. I went to his room in the dorms. He was man enough to cry. I didn't give him one ounce of advice that could help at the time, but I was there and he knew I cared. I don't know where he is today. Yet he knows he's the one I'm talking about—and he knows that it helped him to have me there.

Or ask at what single moment a student did the most to help me in turn, and I think of a time when I came home dejected from a series of meetings that seemed wordy and mean. I sat in the library of my house, wondering why I stayed at this work. A student came in. He had had no contact with those meetings and had no reason so far as I know to be aware that I was thinking of chucking it all. He said only one thing and left: "I think you're doing a great job." I know where he is today. He knows he's the one I'm talking about—and he knows it helped me to have him there.

Haverford prepared me for the lesson about little things in my first days on the job. As I drove down from New York City on the day when I was to start the job, I thought ahead to the kinds of first decisions I'd be called on to make. I fancied myself saving a professor from the right-wing attacks of a suburban Philadelphia foe or the left-wing attacks of a center Philadelphia foe. I saw myself turning down a million-dollar gift because it came with strings attached that were unacceptable to free, inquiring minds. I imagined that in one bold, inspired stroke I would reshape the curriculum with such finesse that the faculty and students alike would hail my skill.

I arrived just before the Labor Day weekend in 1967. The two senior officers, the provost and the vice-president for business, were about to take off for that last holiday before the new year's agitated pace began. I was clearly in charge of the place. But the campus was so calm and the sun so warm that I put on my bathing suit and stretched out in a deckchair behind the house. My first decision could wait.

I slept only a short while. A faculty wife and her sister-in-law, both very agitated in a Quakerly way, came into the yard. The first woman's husband had just returned from a long motor trip that day, had gone over to his office on his bicycle, and had promptly been thrown by a new chain which the college had strung across one of the campus paths. But these women hadn't come for sympathy, even though the professor was now in a hospital bed. They had come for action. That chain must be taken away. I turned at once into the decision-maker I had hoped to be. I looked up the number of the college in the telephone directory, dialed, and left word that the chain was to come down at once. The facts that I was leaving the message with the answering service and that nobody would get it for two days, if at all, were mere details then. I had still shown who was in charge.

The incident was prophetic. Certainly there are far more decisions like that on my record than there are ones of sweeping size. And a tone is set in those little things that may make the few big decisions possible.

Saturday, April 14

The last day on this job was an uncommonly good one to be alive, to be able to work, and to have work to do. The weather was gentle and warm after an early morning temperature at the freezing point.

Steve and I pulled the route alone, and not a thing went wrong. Today the yards and cans all looked familiar to me. I had been into all of them at least once, and into some of them twice. I felt at home in the yards even if no one knew or cared about my name. Who comes twice a week doesn't matter to the people here, but the fact that someone comes matters a lot.

I realized as I went through the yards how much folklore about Dryden I had stored in my head. Once I would have thought that the way to study the sociology of suburban America was through a library, doorstep interviews, and meetings of the P.T.A. Now I know how much of interest is revealed in the town's waste. We pull the trash from about 430 houses a day. That yields twenty cubic yards, or approximately six tons. With a two-man crew, that means I haul three tons of valuable research data a day.

I know now that Dryden, Maryland, A.D. 1973, is a place where:

—Beer is consumed in staggering quantities, but hard liquor is rare and expensive liquor still rarer. The wines don't often get beyond Chianti or the Gallo line.

—Almost everybody buys groceries at the Giant store. Giant uses a fine quality of paper bag.

—For every housebroken dog, there is one in training. There is no general rule about how to dispose of the training materials. It is simply a matter of the householders' consciences and the likelihood that anyone in the family will have to meet the trashman face to face when he is emptying the cans. All dogs are expected to bark at us. If someone wants to find us on the route, he can pinpoint our location at once by the intensity of the barks.

—Nearly everybody reads *The Washington Post,* and many read the *Star* too. The Dryden paper is not a big seller, even though it wraps rather well.

—Shoes appear to be on the way out, if one judges by the discards this week.

—The volume of trash rises with the square of the family income. Thus the very rich need more pickups just to avoid drowning in it. This is what social justice means.

Alexander Pope may be wrong. The proper study of mankind may not be man at all but his trash.

The weather today brought out the best in Dryden. Some people still ignored the greetings I continued to give. But I thought I heard a few more people speak in reply, and speak a little more warmly too.

A six-year-old taunted me as I came into his yard. "Garbageman, garbageman, dirty old truck," he called out in a singsong way, much to the delight of the young girl he was with. He was taken aback by the fact that I replied in a friendly way. He decided to do the same.

"Hey, garbageman, guess what I got for my birthday."

I guessed right. The tricycle on which he rode was clearly new. He rode along as I pulled the trash from his house and the one next door. By now, he had forgotten the girl. We kept up a stream of talk all the time. We were getting to be friends.

"Garbageman, I'm going to ask you to my party for kids and grownups next Tuesday."

That one line made the day, and the week, for

me. I thought how surprised his mother would be if I came and brought the truck. But, as Steve pointed out, we could give her a hand by carting away the wrappings and scraps when it was time for us to go home.

We were back at the garage by 2:00. Neither of us dared to say how well the truck was doing until we were safely out of the cab at last; to talk of our luck might be to drive it away.

I punched the clock, got in my car, and drove out of the yard. The dust swirled in back of my car, but the air ahead was clear.

Sunday, April 15

These days are done. I suppose I should have unmixed emotions about going home, but I don't. No matter how restless I am to get back to my desk, I know too that some day I'll want to do again just what I've done this spring—or perhaps move to fulfill some other half-formed dream. Whatever comes, I expect to do a better job at home because I got away.

The Hasidic rabbi Zusia said, "When I shall face the celestial tribunal, I shall not be asked why I was not Abraham, Jacob, or Moses. I shall be asked why I was not Zusia."

Once, I thought I was leaving my identity behind when I set out on this leave. Now I think I may even have found some part of it along the way.